MAKING BREAD AT HOME

50 recipes from around the world

MAKING BREAD AT HOME

50 recipes from around the world

TOM JAINE

PHOTOGRAPHS BY
JACQUI HURST

CASSELLPAPERBACKS

Text © Tom Jaine, 1995
Photographs © George Weidenfeld & Nicolson Ltd, 1995

First published in 1995 by George Weidenfeld & Nicolson Ltd

First published in paperback in 1997 by Phoenix Illustrated

This paperback edition first published in 2001 by
Cassell Paperbacks, Cassell & Co
Wellington House, 125 Strand
London, WC2R 0BB

British Library Cataloguing-in-Publication Data
A catalogue record for this book is available from
the British Library

ISBN 1841881600

Edited by Felicity Jackson
Designed by Thumb Design
Printed and bound in Italy

CONTENTS

BREAD PAST AND PRESENT

Bread is a staple food, and has been ever since the time when man ceased hunting game and gathering wild plants and took instead to sowing crops and harvesting them. Not every society in the world grew wheat corn and its relatives, the essential ingredient for bread: more people depend on rice, for example, than on wheat; and the whole of north and central America before the Europeans discovered it ran on maize.

However, for those who lived in the Middle East, north Asia and Europe, bread was the thing. As history has turned out, it was from these regions that some of the great modern migrations - of peoples, political power, and economic influence - have originated.

Throughout all of these great historical changes, bread has travelled in the saddle-pack, so that it too has colonized great tracts of the Americas, Africa, Australia and south Asia.

Watching the making of a simple chapati, or the mass production of a loaf of white bread, we take for granted some tremendous leaps of human invention and discovery, each in their way as momentous as the capturing of fire and heat, and as lost in the mists of time.

To make bread you need flour; to get flour you need a mill and a field full of grain, which means agriculture and sophisticated grinding technology. To get risen bread you need yeasts, and these must have taken centuries of haphazard trial and error to tame and make reliable. And finally, to bake you need ovens, no small detail.

Without each of these steps, any one of which speaks generations of development, you are left with simple porridges and gruels - grains mixed with water and boiled.

Even a Mexican tortilla, the griddle bread made from maize by the Aztecs and the Maya, now spread through fast-fooderies in the USA and increasingly in Europe, conceals infinite pains. Easy to make, isn't it, a flat disc of corn (maize) quickly cooked on a hotplate? Yet to get that, the ancient Mexican peoples had to work out how to treat their kernels of corn with limewater to soften the husks, and to boil the starch to make a fresh paste that could be converted into paper-thin tortillas. They also happened on the fact that if they dried this paste, they could regrind it into a flour that would keep all winter long - and that too would make tortillas. Bread is not as simple as it seems.

16th-century French woodcut showing a baker with his ovens. In the background, on the left, an apprentice is loading an oven with raised pies; the baker himself is using his peel to load small rolls, perhaps manchets, while larger round loaves are proving in the warmth of the oven on the right. His immediate helper can be seen weighing pieces of dough for the rolls and moulding them into balls two-handed - just as moulding is done today.

GRAINS

You can't make a loaf without some flour: wheat, rye, barley or oats, the four essentials that have been grown in Europe and Asia for this purpose - with wheat the king - though pea and bean flour, chestnut, rice and potato have also been recruited to help things along in times of famine, not to mention breads made with tree bark or acorns.

The grains that are harvested today are the result of much care. Ancient farmers were not so lucky, making do with primitive forms - single-row barley, emmer, einkorn and spelt, the latter still grown in marginal climates - from which we have selected and refined certain characteristics.

WHEAT

The most effective grain for breadmaking is wheat, not only because it tastes good - a certain nuttiness, no bitterness, and with a round, sometimes rich flavour - but because it performs well. An ear of wheat has all the ingredients for a good loaf: starch to give bulk, feed the yeasts, and turn a lovely golden brown in the oven; germ to lend essential fats and oils, and improve bread's nutritional value; bran to lend weight and help our digestion; and gluten, that magic component possessed by wheat more than any other grain, which lets the loaf stretch and rise to perfection.

Wheats vary from one breed, one harvest and one location to another. Gluten, which is a protein, is one of the essential variants. Wheats grown in hot, dry summers over a short season, i.e. sown in the spring and harvested three or four months later, contain more protein than those from cooler places, which may sow their crops in the winter to give a better chance of ripening. Hence wheat from the prairies of North America, the plains of Hungary in Central Europe, the northern provinces of India, or Australia is particularly blessed with protein. The gluten content is high, and loaves will rise better and be lighter. This is called hard wheat, and it makes a strong flour.

European wheats, with the exception of the durum wheats in Italy used for pasta making, were mainly softer than this, their flour was weaker. A soft flour is ideal for making pastry and cakes, where you do not want a chewy texture. When bread is made with them, it will tend to be denser and less refined. The big advantage of soft wheat, however, is its flavour. It simply has more. The hearty country loaves of

France illustrate these points perfectly. But when a French baker wanted something more dainty, he would often use imported flour.

The position today has been changed by chemists and agricultural science. European wheats, through careful breeding, are no longer so soft as they were; and bakers and millers can alter their performance by adding pure gluten and other improvers. But it is still worth finding a bag of 100% American strong flour just to see the remarkable properties of spring wheat from the prairies.

A selection of the flours available for making bread. Top row, left to right: 85% organic brown, 100% organic wholemeal, unbleached organic white, strong white bread flour. Bottom row left to right: maize meal (polenta), barley flour, organic rye, chapati flour.

OTHER GRAINS

Rye is an excellent bread corn. It has a fine flavour, and sufficient gluten (although not very much) to rise in the making. Rye loaves will always be denser than wheaten, and nowadays almost every baker mixes in some wheat to help with the texture. In the Middle Ages, these were called maslin loaves. Rye is particularly favoured in Germany and countries to the north and east of it, although recipes for rye loaves have survived from most marginal regions, for instance the Alpine slopes of the Italian Tirol, or the moist maritime province of Galicia in north-western Spain.

Where rye is appreciated, the sourdough system of bread fermentation is almost universal. This is part science, part history, part taste. Natural sour fermentations (they are called lactic) are obviously to the liking of all these peoples, think of sauerkraut in Germany, sour cream in Russia, soured or pickled herrings in Scandinavia, and rye seems to have an affinity with a slightly sharp flavour.

Barley makes an enjoyable bread, but does not have the gluten necessary to make it light like wheat. It is an ancient grain, primitive versions of it have been found on sites in Bulgaria that yield evidence of the earliest full-scale bakers in Europe. It also can cope with extremes of wet and cold, so was popular with farmers in lands like Scotland and the far west of Britain. Barley bread is uncommon nowadays.

Another grain that fares well in poor soils and climates is oats but, like barley, it has mostly disappeared from the modern baker's repertoire. Its principle use was for flatbreads in regions like the north of England and Scotland, though it was also an important element in the multigrain breads of Germany, Poland and European Russia. It has no gluten, so needs to be mixed with wheat for a risen loaf.

Countries beyond Europe have converted other grains and staples into breads or foods that are directly comparable to bread in their place in a society's diet. The maize of America is the most obvious example, not only providing the raw material for tortillas and other Indian breads, but adopted with enthusiasm by European settlers for their Johnnycakes and cornbreads, and exported back to their homelands where the crop grew well in zones not blessed with good wheat: hence polenta of northern Italy, mamaliga of Rumania, and the cornbreads of Spain and Portugal.

BREAD BAKER'S UTENSILS

An English baker's equipment, at the end of the 19th century

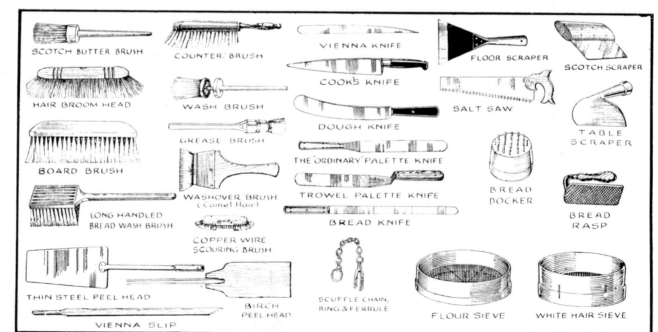

SCOTCH BUTTER BRUSH

COUNTER BRUSH

VIENNA KNIFE

FLOOR SCRAPER

SCOTCH SCRAPER

HAIR BROOM HEAD

WASH BRUSH

COOK'S KNIFE

SALT SAW

BOARD BRUSH

GREASE BRUSH

DOUGH KNIFE

TABLE SCRAPER

THE ORDINARY PALETTE KNIFE

BREAD DOCKER

WASHOVER BRUSH (Camel Hair)

TROWEL PALETTE KNIFE

BREAD RASP

LONG HANDLED BREAD WASH BRUSH

COPPER WIRE SCOURING BRUSH

BREAD KNIFE

THIN STEEL PEEL HEAD

BIRCH PEEL HEAD

SCUFFLE CHAIN, RING & FERRULE

FLOUR SIEVE

WHITE HAIR SIEVE

VIENNA SLIP

MILLING THE FLOUR

If grains are to be used in cooking, they need to be ground to a flour. Once human numbers expanded beyond units of a few self-sufficient families, the amount of flour needed to keep everyone from hunger was vastly greater than could be turned out by women at home pounding away in a mortar.

The development of primitive flour-milling involves the shift from the up-and-down crushing of the pestle and mortar to a flat, scraping movement as the bowl of the mortar was opened into a flatter form, and the pestle became a two-handed flat stone which was rubbed back and forth across the grain, the flour collecting in a hollow at the end.

A to and fro movement was easier work if converted to round and round. If the bottom stone was made slightly conical, and the top stone revolved round its tip this was faster and less back-breaking. If grooves were cut in the stone, it increased the shearing effect. This simple rotary handmill was the essence of all a mill needed to be.

Such querns, as they are called, were found in the eastern Mediterranean from early classical times; the contribution of the great urban cultures of Greece and Rome was to make these stones, originally operated by two women sitting opposite each other, bigger and faster. Slaves, donkeys and oxen were made to turn very large mills. Then the brilliant leap was made to using water to drive a wheel which turned the stones. Water mills meant that stones could be larger and flatter, because the power was so much greater. This brought the possibility of fine flour within the grasp of any community near a mill. Wind power came much later, in about AD 1000.

Corn ground between stones was either left as wholemeal, none of the bran extracted, or could be passed through sieves of papyrus, horsehair or linen of differing fineness to produce flour that was more or less white.

Production of very white flour was made easier when steel roller mills were developed in the 1820s. Multiple rollers ground, or rather pressed the grain, so separating the bran, germ and endosperm. But objections to roller milling persist. It operates too fast, generating heat which damages enzymes in the flour; it creates a characterless, and nutritionally inert flour by excluding important components, particularly the germ; it makes a nonsense of the concept of 'wholemeal' by removing the various fractions, then adding them back in at the end of the milling process. Stoneground flours are often preferred by people who take their bread seriously.

An emblematic representation of a French baker of the 18th century. Different shapes of loaves, rolls and pretzels are hung about his person, and he has a baker's peel in one hand, a brush for sweeping the counter and the bottoms of loaves in the other. In the background, one baker is kneading dough in a stone trough, while the other is charging a behive oven - in this case with a separate hearth.

11

LEAVENING AND BAKING

Proving baskets from the beginning of this century. One is for long loaves, the other for rings. French proving baskets are lined with linen; some other baskets are made with fine wicker and need no separate lining, merely thorough dusting with flour.

If you make a paste of flour and water, and cook it straight away, the result is a pancake or a lump of dough like the Australian bush food, damper. Bread, perhaps, but it does not answer most of our requirements of a loaf. This is because it is unleavened.

Some means had to be discovered, before we get to the point of our 'simple' loaf of bread to fill it with gas and transform it from a tasty morsel to an intricate network of starch and air. That means was fermentation: the natural process of maturation that causes little bubbles of air in a fermenting fluid like beer or wine, or in something even simpler like a paste of flour and water. The discovery of this too has been laid at the door of the ancient Egyptians.

It was probably by accident when a batch of dough became infected by the wild yeast spores which float in the air. If, for reasons of economy, the apparently spoilt, sour-tasting and rotten dough was baked anyway, it would have been realized that the bread was lighter and had a special, good flavour. Later came the thought that a piece of leavened dough could be kept to spread the infection to the next batch.

When the Israelites fled from Egypt in the Exodus they left their leaven behind; unlike the more provident prospectors of the American west who carried their cultures with them, hence San Francisco sourdoughs. The Israelites

Fig. 19.—Basket for Proving Ring Loaves

thereafter had to exist on unleavened bread. This was the origin of the Passover bread matzot. But unleavened bread continued in use in many societies. The Romans, especially old-fashioned ones in the early days of the Empire, felt that it was traditional, correct and healthier - the newfangled

leavened doughs an import from luxurious Greece.

Ultimately, the Romans did borrow the use of ale-barm or brewers' yeast, from subjected Germanic tribes.

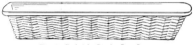

Fig. 18.—Basket for Proving Long Loaves

The breads of some societies have relied mainly on lactic fermentation - which is the base of the whole family of sourdoughs - while others, especially the British Isles, have long depended on straight alcoholic fermentations using brewers' yeast. An inhibiting factor in the adoption of brewers' yeast was its availability: it could not survive extremes of heat, and not all communities had alcohol on the bubble week in, week out.

EARLY OVENS

The first breads were cooked on flat stones heated directly in the fire. This principle of the griddle or bakestone continues to operate wherever flatbreads like chapatis, bannocks or tortillas are still the daily diet. It doesn't work, however, if you want to bake: that needs an oven.

It was a natural step to cover the stone with an inverted pot to contain the heat. The domed beehive oven, a freestanding structure with its own source of heat, is the same idea, but on a larger scale. Early examples have been found in Mesopotamia, Egypt and the Balkans, and it was this pattern that spread throughout Europe and the Near East.

The beehive oven is heated by burning a fire on its floor. The flames exit through the door itself or, later, through internal chimneys. When the fire has heated the structure, it is raked out and the risen dough put in its place. The doorway is sealed, and the bread cooks in a falling heat radiating from every surface, the oven space capturing and recycling any moisture that evaporates from the loaves.

Technical development of ovens did not quicken pace until the 18th century when improvements in design allowed the more efficient retention, or even introduction, of moisture - hence the crackling thin crusts of Viennese and, eventually, Parisian loaves - and led to methods of remote heating rather than burning fuel on the oven floor.

Since the 19th century, there have been lots of changes in the detail of an oven's design: what it is made from, how it is heated, and so on, but the principles have not really varied until they began to make ovens that had bread moving through them on conveyor belts, so that the air was being heated, but not really the floor and walls. This is getting very close to steaming the bread, something we in England and America know only too well, to our regret. It makes for a faster loaf, but not necessarily better tasting. However, if you were a baker trying to provide essential food to a population counted in millions, many of whom were unwilling to pay very much, you too would turn to industrial processes.

In Greece and the Near East, the village baker cooked bread fashioned in the homes of his customers, as well as baking joints of meat after the first heat had gone off, just as did his equivalents in other countries.

COMMUNAL OVENS

Although ovens can be built any size, there are advantages of time in having them fairly large. The same may be said of mills. Hence bread baking has often appeared a communal activity to avoid duplication of expensive resources. Grain is ground at the village mill; dough is baked in an oven, owned either by the community, or in the hands of a tradesman who gains his living therefrom.

PROFESSIONAL BAKERS

The nature of bread production - that it should usually be on a larger scale than that of other foods - also gave rise to its early organization into a professional trade. Full-time bakers are identifiable from the records of ancient Egypt and there are scores of references to them in Athenian comedies. In Rome there was a bakers' guild from approximately 150 BC; in medieval London and Paris, bakers' guilds were among the earliest craft brotherhoods.

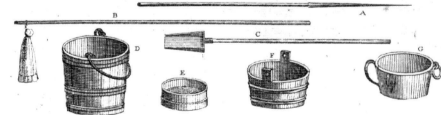

A French print of the late 18th century depicting a bakery. On the upper floor is the dough trough and kneading board, as well as sacks of flour; below the oven is being stoked, with wood stored for drying in the cupboard below the oven floor. Buckets, measures, a sieve, a peel and a scuffle for swabbing out the oven after the fire has been raked out are illustrated at the bottom of the picture.

ESSENTIAL TECHNIQUES

Anyone can make a loaf of bread. It is not a difficult art. However, there is great mystique about the magic of yeast and fermentation, and that's fair comment, it is a magical process. At the same time, however, it is a transformation within everyone's grasp.

Most of the skill of baking is about routine and regularity, with a refusal to take short cuts added to the recipe. The ingredients are few in number: just flour, water, salt and yeast or leaven for most essential breads. These behave in predictable ways, so if you follow the rules, bread will result. Better bread comes from repetition.

Imagine the timetable of a professional baker. If there's no bread in the shop by opening time, he won't make a living. If the croissants are not baked before breakfast, when will they ever be eaten? To make sure he keeps to time, he imposes a strict pattern on his work. The dough is mixed to the same recipe; it ferments at the same temperature; the ovens are set at identical heat to yesterday.

He will have to cope with variations - flour may differ from year to year, the weather and humidity will alter the condition of the dough - but he must know what is happening in order to meet that deadline. As if that were not enough, the baker also has the law to deal with. Each loaf must be the same size, or penalties result. Customers never like to feel cheated. And so the weighing of the pieces of dough works again to a pattern, regularity is all.

The home baker need not worry about weights and measures inspectors, nor even public health regulations, but he or she will do well to follow the same discipline as the tradesman. If you don't know what you have just done, you will never learn by experience and be able to correct your mistakes. Some people keep notes, others rely on good memories. Once you understand it, bread is quite even-tempered: it will accept delays, it will not invariably ruin because you had to run an errand, as long as you don't abuse it, and you know when to stop and devote your whole attention to it.

PREPARING A NATURAL LEAVEN AND YEASTED STARTER

Leavening in bread dough is the extra ingredient that makes a loaf so enjoyable, be it an Ethiopian injera, or a large Italian country bread.

Leavening lightens dough by introducing air. If you beat eggs into a cake mixture, you incorporate air by the beating action, which the egg white holds and traps by its physical composition. The expanded batter is then set in the heat of the oven. Or you can add chemicals: bicarbonate of soda, cream of tartar, or baking powder. Here, chemical interaction between substances generates gas for a short time which can be sealed into the dough by cooking.

FERMENTATION

The way that bread is usually lightened is through some sort of fermentation. Fermentation produces gas and heat in many food substances if you leave them for long enough in the atmosphere. Not all fermentation is a good thing: a stockpot that fizzes in the larder usually needs throwing away, because it is 'off'; but some sorts are recognized to do us no harm and to taste nice into the bargain. Milk that ferments turns into yoghurt and cheese. Juices and extracts that ferment are transformed into beer, cider and wine. Vegetables that ferment keep all the winter long (how else could they store them without deep-freezes) and are served at table as sauerkraut or Korean kimchee.

NATURAL LEAVEN

In a bread dough, flour mixed with water creates a gently sour taste in a lactic fermentation, souring like milk - not alcoholic, turning ultimately to vinegar, which is what happens in a yeast-driven fermentation.

This natural fermentation creates air and generates heat which further expands the gas. The trick of bread is to mix a fresh dough that can be worked on by a prepared ferment and, lo, a finished loaf! The loaf is conditioned by our working it through mixing and kneading, and it is expanded or raised by the gas of the ferment, and everything is set by the heat of the oven.

Early bakers relied on this spontaneous leaven. It gives a more or less sour taste which often seems to enhance that of the flour. By constant repetition, and keeping the leaven renewed from one day to the next, they built in a degree of reliability. This system is still used by the bakers of France, Germany and many parts of eastern Europe, as well as Americans making San Francisco sourdough.

YEASTED STARTER

The other important form of leavening is brewers' yeast. A natural leaven has wild yeasts in it. They inhabit the air, wherever we turn, and will settle on your ferment and start breeding. Yeast is a fungus that multiplies at enormous speed in the right conditions. Gas and heat are the result of this fast-breeder. Yeasts that just settle are usually wild, weak and unpredictable: they enhance but do not overpower the spontaneous lactic fermentation of flour and water.

Brewers' yeast, which is a particularly strong form, is a by-product of brewing and wine-making. Bakers found (as early as the ancient Romans) that using brewers' yeast was a fast way of leavening, and more reliable than a spontaneous fermentation. Some societies have been using it ever since.

I always use fresh yeast as it gives the best flavour and is ready to use immediately, so all the recipes in this book use fresh yeast. It is available from bakers, health food shops and specialist shops, and comes as a brown, compressed lump which crumbles easily. It can be stored, wrapped in a plastic bag, in the refrigerator for up to 2 weeks.

Dried yeast can be substituted for fresh, if preferred. Use half the weight of dried yeast as the weight of fresh yeast specified in the ingredients.

Easy-blend dried yeast can also be used, follow the manufacturer's instructions for the quantity to use.

TO MAKE A SOURDOUGH LEAVEN

Natural leavens take a few days to get going. They need to be kept in a warm room and out of draughts. If it is too cold, they will take very much longer to ripen, and then taste too sour. Luckily for us, they keep well in a refrigerator. If you want to start a leaven and use it once a week, you can pinch off a piece of dough weighing approximately 225 g/8 oz from the finished dough when you have made it, pop it in a glass bowl, cover it with clingfilm and store it in the refrigerator. A day or two before you want to bake, take up the recipe below from the point of the second refreshment.

The starter
* *60 g/2 oz wholemeal flour (wheat or rye depending on the sort of loaf you want)*
* *30 ml/1 fl oz spring or boiled water (chlorine in water supplies is best avoided)*

Mix to a paste the flour and water and knead it with your fingers and thumbs until it is a smooth, firm dough.

Put this nut of dough in a glass or small bowl, cover it with a cheese cloth (not clingfilm) and leave it in a warm place, at approximately 24-26°C/75-80°F, for about 2 days.

Although the outside will crust over, the inside will be moist and slightly aerated. The smell will be sweet.

Discard the crust and proceed with the first refreshment.

The first refreshment

* 60 ml / 2 fl oz spring or boiled water
* 120 g / 4 oz wholemeal flour

Dissolve the starter in the water, add the flour and mix to a dough. Knead with the fingers on a work table.

Put the dough in a small bowl and cover with clingfilm. Put it back in your warm spot and leave for a day or two. It will crust again, but it will also have enlarged, and the aeration will be greater. The smell will be very slightly sharp.

Discard the crust and proceed with the second refreshment.

The second refreshment

* 120 ml / 4 fl oz spring or boiled water
* 225 g / 8 oz unbleached white bread flour

Repeat as for the first refreshment, but this time leave it for about 8-12 hours and it should show every sign of life: growing and rising like a normal piece of dough with a slightly sharp edge to the smell, but not rotten or 'off'.

The leaven is now ready to be added to a dough which will proceed as any other, though often more slowly.

The recipes I have given that use leavens, for instance French Country Bread (see page 30) or the German Sourdough Rye Bread (see page 76), give instructions from almost the very beginning of the process.

TO MAKE A BIGA (YEASTED STARTER)

The Italian biga is a piece of matured dough with a speck of yeast in it. It gives loaves a more interesting texture than they would get from a simple yeast dough ripened for only a few hours.

* 225 g / 8 oz unbleached white plain flour
* 7 g / 1/4 oz fresh yeast
* 90 ml / 3 fl oz tepid water

Make a well in the middle of the flour, crumble in the yeast and add the water. Mix to cream the yeast, then extend the mixing to incorporate the flour.

Mix until all the dry flour has been taken up, then knead on a work surface to a stiff and smooth dough. Leave in a bowl covered with clingfilm overnight (12 hours or more) at a temperature not less than 21°C/70°F.

It should rise once and fall back again before being used for a bread dough as detailed in the recipes for Ciabatta (see page 44), Italian Country Bread (see page 48) and North Italian Rye Bread (see page 51).

Left: The ingredients for a biga (yeasted starter) are fresh yeast, flour and water.
Right: Mix the flour, yeast and liquid until all the dry flour has been taken up.

MIXING

Mixing the dough happens when you first combine all the weighed and measured ingredients. It sounds very simple, but what is done at this stage will sometimes affect the outcome of your ideal loaf.

Take care to follow the recipe's instructions about starting the mix: sometimes a leaven or starter is dissolved in water; sometimes flour and salt are mixed dry, a well is made in the centre, then yeast is crumbled into the well and water is added; sometimes yeast is creamed in water or milk and added as a liquor to the flour.

Sugar used to be a constant ingredient in bread recipes, but modern yeasts do not usually need sugar to help them become active.

Mixing gets all the dry ingredients evenly wetted. If you are mixing a big batch of dough, this is more difficult than it may seem - the last scraps of flour take a long time to be incorporated. The mixing should, therefore, be done with generous sweeps of the hand (this is usually better than using a spoon), making sure that you get the water to all the corners, so that all the flour is mixed in.

Mix the liquid into the flour with your hand, this is usually better than a spoon when mixing large amounts.

TEMPERATURE OF THE LIQUID

Yeast will die if it is overheated (say above 50°C/120°F) and will be slowed or dormant if the temperature is too low. If you add boiling hot water to a dough, you will probably kill the yeast and nothing will rise. If you add stone-cold liquor, then the yeasts will take correspondingly longer to become active - 25°C/77°F is their ideal operating temperature.

The temperature of the water will therefore depend on how fast you want the dough to develop. Sourdoughs are more sensitive than bakers' yeast. If you keep them too cool, they will move too slowly.

The home baker does not need to worry too much about temperature, though the professional must do so, otherwise his bread will take a variable amount of time to ripen and so may miss the first rush of customers. There are some recipes - wholemeal bread, rye sourdough, or Vienna loaves, where temperature matters, whether keeping the dough warm all the time, or keeping it cool.

ADDING FATS AND OTHER INGREDIENTS

The mixing is also the time that fats and other ingredients are added to doughs. Small quantities of hard fat or oil are no problem. Rub butter into the flour at the outset, or add it melted after the water. Add oil with the water. Some fat helps make the crumb more tender, just as will using milk instead of water. But if a lot of fat is to be incorporated, remember that the fat will coat the particles of flour and stop the yeast fungus getting to the starch sugars which are its food. A rich bun or brioche recipe, therefore, should give the yeast a period of time alone with the flour before the fat is added. Such doughs are often made in two stages: a sponge of flour, yeast and water, and the fat added later.

Spices may be added to the dough in various ways. For instance, saffron is added to Cornish Saffron Bread (see page 63) by making an infusion which is then mixed with the yeast and liquid before being added to the flour, with Russian Black Bread (see page 90) spices are added to the molasses and yeast. In others, such as French Spice Bread (see page 40), spices are added after the flour and honey have been mixed.

Additions of solid ingredients - currants, raisins, olives or nuts, for example - will usually be made after the dough has been mixed and given a first bout of kneading. A large quantity of fruit or something similar will only get in the way of working the dough.

Some recipes specify that fruit such as raisins and sultanas should be warmed slightly before they are scattered over the surface of the dough.

DRY DOUGH

If you feel the dough is too dry, it can be a problem adding more water at the end of mixing. Sometimes you can add a bit more moisture by constantly wetting your hands during the first stages of kneading.

Other times, it can be easier to mix a little extra cold water with some flour to make a smooth paste and then mix that into the dough.

Mix the dough with generous sweeps of the hand, getting the water to all the corners, so the dry ingredients are evenly wetted.

KNEADING

Once the dough has been mixed, it must be kneaded. While mixing combines all the ingredients, kneading conditions them. The key to good bread is conditioning the gluten in the wheat flour.

Wheat flour consists mainly of starch, which gives the loaf its bulk, and gluten, a protein that forms long thin strands to support the weight of starch when the dough is kneaded, and trapping tiny balloons of gas in the dough, preventing them escaping - without gluten a loaf of bread would not be light.

You can see gluten in its raw state if you form a ball of flour and water and hold it in a sieve under running water. Soon, the starch is washed off leaving a dense white bean of gluten, for all the world like a piece of chewing gum: stretchy, elastic and enduring.

Kneading activates the gluten, making the strands longer and stronger.

Wheat flour has the most gluten; rye contains less, yet has some natural gums, so remains sticky during kneading and makes a denser loaf. Barley and other grains like maize have little or none and need wheat flour added to them to hold a loaf shape at all.

Kneading should be done on a clean, flat surface, dusted with flour to keep the dough from sticking. Scrape the dough from the mixing bowl and begin by pressing the heel of one hand firmly into the mass. Push through to stretch it, then lift the leading edge back over to make a ball once more.

Swivel the ball through one quarter of a turn and press again with the heel of the hand, fold and turn. Repeating these movements rhythmically, watch the untidy mixture of flour and water convert into a supple, lithe cushion of satin-smooth, elastic bread dough.

HOW LONG TO KNEAD

There is no absolute rule about how long to knead or how many 'turns' to give the dough, it depends on feel. Hard

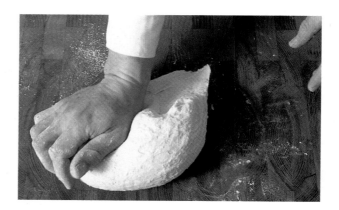

flours require more work, they will stay grainy in texture for longer. It is usually thought that 10 minutes of vigorous hand kneading is sufficient. A soft brown flour will probably take only half that time.

KNEADING IN A BOWL

Some doughs are too moist and runny to be worked on the table at all. An enriched dough made with butter and eggs will often be kneaded in a bowl. Other doughs are kneaded in the bowl before being turned on to the work surface.

Working with moist doughs is one of the aspects of baking that separates the seasoned practitioner from beginners: 'Oh! this is far too wet', is a cry often heard at first. But if the dough is kneading by a punching action with thumb and fist in the bowl, then stretched like gum before punching again, it is possible to condition the dough sufficiently to bring it on to the table without vast quantities of flour to stop it sticking.

If a dough is moist, work fast, use the scraper to keep the table clean, and keep your hands clean. Rye doughs present another problem because of natural pentosans making it gluey. Cleanliness helps, so do wet hands.

When the kneaded dough is supple and elastic, shape it into a smooth ball ready for rising.

RISING

Once the dough has been mixed and kneaded, it is ready for the first rise, when the yeast or other raising agent does its work through fermentation creating carbon dioxide gas which is trapped in the dough by the elastic web of gluten. By stretching the gluten in this way, it conditions the flour - gives it exercise. The fermentation process also causes various changes to starches and enzymes in the flour, further conditioning it.

RISING TEMPERATURE

Usually, dough is left to rise in a warm place, such as an airing cupboard, with a temperature of 24-26°C/75-80°F. Warmth is not essential, but it speeds the process. Although a cold fermentation may be no bad thing, draughts are not so good and play havoc with even development; and too much heat starts to 'cook' the bread.

What is essential is that the dough should be kept airtight so a skin does not form on top. The best thing is to place the dough in a clean bowl with a tight wrap of clingfilm over the top of the bowl, or press oiled clingfilm on the dough itself. A damp tea towel placed over the bowl is another way, but not so effective.

LENGTH OF TIME

How long a dough needs to rise depends on how much yeast or leaven is used and the temperature it is kept at. Some are left in the cool overnight, others take under 2 hours. Usually the first rise sees the dough double in size, occasionally treble. The time in fermentation will have some result on the taste and texture of a bread. A simple axiom, proved only by exceptions, is that the slower the ripening of a dough, the better the taste. Wheat has a flavour, but it is difficult to capture. Time is the key.

A long fermentation will probably also imply a small quantity of yeast. This too is good for flavour - the flour is not overpowered by the taste of yeast - and is very good for a long life to a bread. Highly yeasted breads do not keep long, nor do short process ones unless additives are thrown into the recipe to delay staling. A leaven bread, using a different form of fermentation and wild yeasts plus a scrap of brewers' yeast, keeps for several days.

KNOCKING BACK

Some bread recipes specify that the dough should rest in two or even three stages, and should be 'knocked back' after each stage before it is finally shaped or moulded.

This process, where you deflate the risen dough with your fist, and fold it over on itself to recommence the process, has the effect of redistributing the gases created by fermentation, of spreading the yeast through new parts of the dough where it can find more food from the flour, and actually redoubling its activity. This helps to ensure an even texture in the bread.

The subsequent rise is usually faster than the first one. A multi-stage rise seems often to make the bread lighter, as if exercise makes the gluten stretch further.

Above: *Place the dough in a bowl, cover it with oiled clingfilm and leave to rise in a warm place, such as an airing cupboard.*

Left: *At the end of the rising time, the dough will have doubled in size.*

23

SHAPING AND PROVING

Once the first rise (or two or three rises, where this is specified) is complete, the dough is returned to the work surface, knocked back and divided, if making more than one loaf, ready for shaping or moulding.

Instructions for shaping individual breads is normally specified in the recipe, but there are some general tips common to most breads.

Do not use too much flour on the work surface at this stage. For one, it will coat the outside of your shape and make it difficult to pinch together to form an undivided whole. For another, this flour has not been conditioned by any kneading and if it is rolled in to a shape, for instance when making a French baguette, it may appear as an unwelcome streak in the finished crumb.

The point of moulding is to produce an unblemished crust on the top of the loaf. If you tear the dough, or stretch it by working too fast or roughly (doughs need to rest between bouts of manipulation, or else the gluten will not stretch smoothly), the crust will be unsightly. This is the reason for sometimes quite detailed suggestions on how to make a shape. A well-moulded loaf, even in a tin, will rise higher than a badly shaped one.

PROVING CONTAINERS

Some breads are cooked in tins or pots, others are placed directly on the oven floor. The first are given their final rise in the containers destined for the oven. Therefore the shape is placed exactly as it will appear in the finished loaf, i.e. with the joins or creases on the underside.

Loaf tins should usually be warmed before placing a loaf in them, otherwise the chill strikes the outside of the loaf and slows the rising at that point. This is one cause of dense bottoms to tin loaves which are yet fully risen on the top. Tins also need seasoning or greasing, and non-stick tins are a life-saver to the home baker. To grease them, wipe vegetable oil over the surface with kitchen roll. Black tins are better than shiny ones. They absorb the heat while shiny metal reflects it, the crusts in black tins will therefore be crisper.

If you wish to bake something like a round loaf or baguette on a baking sheet, you will either have to prove the loaf directly on the baking sheet, or let it rise in a proving basket lined with floured linen - these come in round or long shapes - then turn it on to the baking sheet just before baking. The advantage of using baskets rather than proving directly on baking sheets is that the dough does not get chilled or skinned on the outside.

If you have an oven where you can bake on the floor - or perhaps you have invested in a baking stone which you place in a gas or electric cooker to replicate a baker's oven floor - then you will need to prove in a proving basket, or a floured wicker basket.

If using a proving basket, the loaf must be placed upside down in it to prove. It is then turned on to a baker's peel (a long-handled wooden shovel) to be slashed, before being shot into the oven. You can buy a peel, or you can make one with a broom handle and a piece of thin plywood, or carve one out of a single piece of wood.

KEEPING THE DOUGH WARM

The final proof is the last rise before baking. It does not usually take long, though there are some loaves that are left for more than two, even as much as four, hours. Proving should be done in a warm place (26-29°C/80-85°F) away from draughts. It is important that the outside skin should not crust in the air. Bakers put their loaves in steam-laden proving cupboards, but I use pieces of oiled clingfilm placed directly on the shaped loaf. They are easily removed unless you don't oil them enough, or you leave the loaf too long.

TIMING

It is always difficult to be sure that timing is correct in proving. Do it too little and the loaf will be tight, or else fly away in the oven. Too much, and the whole thing will collapse. Old Russian bakers were advised to prove their white breads in a tub of water. When the shaped loaf rose to the top, it was ready to bake. You can do the same with a lump of dough in a jar of water. Place it next to the loaves you are proving, when it comes to the surface, they too will be ready.

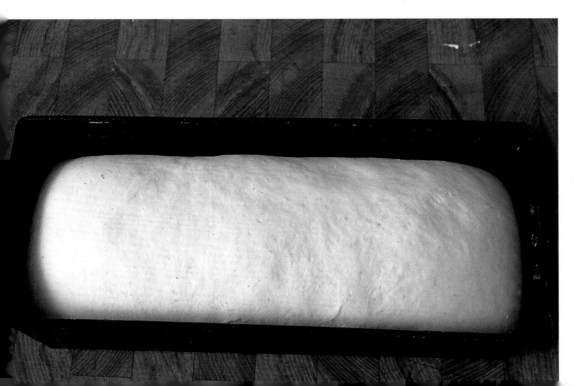

Opposite page: *After the first rise, return the dough to the lightly floured work surface and knock back before shaping or moulding it.*

Above: *The dough is placed in the tin as it will appear in the finished loaf, with the joins or creases on the underside.*

Left: *At the end of the proving time, the shaped dough has almost doubled in size and is puffy in appearance.*

BAKING

The last proof over, the dough has risen, the oven has been heated to the required temperature and all that needs to be done is to slash the loaves or glaze them before they are baked.

Not every bread is slashed before baking, but many are, and for a practical reason. Even a loaf of perfect proof has a last bit of expansion, called 'spring', left in it when exposed to the oven's heat. A loaf that has been underproved will have lots. Only those that have collapsed through overproof will not rise up again, though a really hot and moist oven will sometimes nearly rescue them.

The heat converts moisture into steam and expands the gases trapped in the dough, while the yeast continues to produce carbon dioxide until it is killed by the heat. The centre of a loaf takes a long time to get to the requisite temperature, so rising will carry on until the crust is set (the sugars gelatinized) on the outside and can grow no more.

Slashing or cutting the crust controls the direction, and sometimes the extent, of the spring. Use a serrated knife for slashing the dough - it is easier than a razor, the baker's usual tool. If your loaf is overproved (does not have much spring), cut it only a little; if underproved, slash it long and deep. The patterns are not just for visual effect.

Slash the bread with a knife, to control the direction and extent of the spring during cooking.

MOISTURE IN THE OVEN

Expansion of the crust, and some delay in its setting hard, is also helped by moisture. A baker's oven is completely sealed in a way that a domestic oven is not: moisture evaporating from the loaves is therefore recycled as steam.

However, at home you need to introduce moisture into the oven, either by glazing the loaf (which often helps give the finished loaf a handsome colour) or by spraying water into the oven during the first few minutes of the baking time, using a garden atomizer or the thoroughly-cleaned spray attachment from a household cleaner.

Some people put a roasting tin in the bottom of the oven and pour boiling water in to create steam during the first part of the cooking time.

Cooking in a baker's oven is done on a falling heat. Start hot and cool down. The first rush of heat maximizes that spring, then sets the crust on it and gives a start to the colouring. So at home the oven will be set at maximum, and loaves baked in the upper half. If bread is baked on two shelves, especial care is needed to swap them round to give equal chance of real heat, unless the oven circulates the air.

Major heat may not be needed for all the cooking, and the oven can be turned down for the last half. It is possible that bread baked in tins will have soft crusts in a domestic cooker. They can be removed from the tins and finished in the lower heat to crisp the outsides as well as cook the inside.

Cooking removes moisture from the dough, as well as making a hard crust. When testing to see if a loaf is done, the simplest way is to take it in one hand and tap its bottom with the other. It will sound hollow, and vibrations will travel through the loaf and register on the palm holding the loaf. If not cooked, it will sound utterly dull, with no sympathetic movement. Some loaves are better tested as if they were cakes - insert a fine skewer into the centre and see if it comes out dry and clean.

COOLING

Many breads need cooling. This is partly to allow them to continue to evaporate moisture: if you set a cooked loaf directly on the table it would be heavy and moist where it sat. In the old days of country baking, giant loaves, weighing 6-7 kg/12-14 lb, would be cooked once a week. These would take hours and the crust would get thicker and thicker, tougher and tougher. They would be wrapped in a cloth directly they came out of the oven to soften them. The same is done with some flatbreads, but usually we cool to crispen.

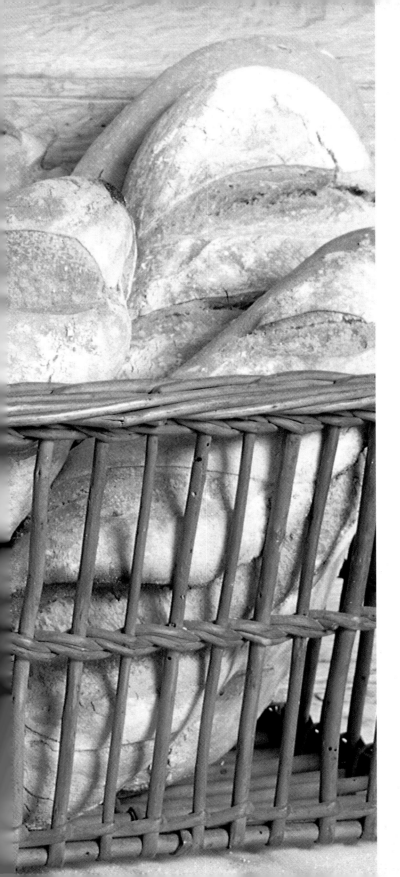

FRENCH BREADS

To some people, France is the home of bread. The baguette or French stick stands in baskets in bakeries the world over, and the heavier, homelier pain de campagne is thought the touchstone of hearty goodness.

There are two traditions at work here. Pain de campagne and many of the older breads are made with a leaven or sourdough (though it is never as sour as a German rye bread, for example) while the more modern types, of which the baguette is the most famous, depend on a long fermentation based on yeast.

Yeast was not approved of by French bakers when it first became current amongst some of their number in the 17th century. It was thought bad for health, and detrimental to a true wheaten flavour, and this opinion has never quite disappeared. So the old way of doing things has never died, even if it has suffered quite a few attacks from industrialization and automation in recent years.

It may be easy to condemn much current French bread as lacking character - simply because everything is done so quickly - but the best of bakers continue to use long fermentation times, whether baking with leaven, yeast or a combination of the two. It is this leisurely timetable that lets the wheat speak.

Clockwise from centre: *Pain Polka, French Country Bread, Baguettes, French Rolls, Walnut Bread and French Hearth Bread.*

FRENCH COUNTRY BREAD

Pain de campagne

The method used in this recipe allows you to make two large loaves of sourdough or leaven bread in easy stages over a period of two days. The process is quite lengthy, but it gets round the problem of regular feeding of leaven that often results in lots of bowls dotted around the kitchen and larder. It's all much simpler in a bakery. There, the routine works steadily round the clock. But not everyone wants to bake daily, or indeed needs to.

This recipe, therefore, needs just one preliminary ingredient - a walnut of leaven, stored in the refrigerator from the last time you made some leaven bread - then takes you through to finished loaves. If you have no leaven at all, see the instructions for making a leaven on page 16.

When proving the loaf, place a nut of the dough in a storage jar or jug filled with water at room temperature. When it rises to the surface, the bread is ready to go in the oven.

Makes 2 large loaves

Day 1: 10.00 am
* *walnut of leaven from previous baking*
* *30 fl oz / 1 fl oz cold water*
* *60 g / 2 oz unbleached white bread flour*

1 Put the leaven in a bowl and mix with the water, then add the flour and knead to a homogenous dough with your fingertips. Put the dough in a small bowl covered with clingfilm and leave to ripen at about 24°C/75°F. It will at least double in size.

Day 1: 5.00 pm
* *100 ml / 3 1/2 fl oz tepid water*
* *the leaven from the previous stage*
* *200 g / 7 oz unbleached white bread flour*

2 Add the water to the leaven to dissolve it, mix in the flour and knead the dough on a floured work surface. Leave it to rise in a bowl covered with clingfilm at about 24°C/75°F. It will at least double in size. It will have a definite smell, vinegary and sharp, but not overly strong.

Day 1: 11.00 pm
* *175 ml / 6 fl oz cold water*
* *the leaven from the previous stage*
* *350 g / 12 oz unbleached white bread flour*

3 Add the water to the leaven to dissolve it, mix in the flour gradually, then knead it on the work surface for 10 minutes. Leave to rise in a bowl covered with clingfilm at 10°C/50°F overnight. It will at least double in size.

Day 2: 8.00 am
* *the leaven from the previous stage*
* *450 ml / 16 fl oz water at 43°C/110°F*
* *800 g / 1 3/4 lb unbleached white plain flour*
* *30 g / 1 oz salt*

4 Make a soup of the leaven and the water, squeezing it between your fingers to break it up. Mix the flour and salt together, then gradually add them to the liquid, mixing the while. Mix to a dough that leaves the sides of the bowl clean, then knead on a floured work surface for 10 minutes, until smooth and resilient. Leave the dough to rise in a bowl covered with clingfilm in a warm place (24°C/75°F) for between 2 and 3 hours, until doubled in size.

5 Turn out the dough on to the lightly floured work surface, knock back, divide in half and mould each piece into a ball. At this stage, take off a walnut of dough to act as leaven for the next time. Put it in a small bowl, cover with clingfilm and refrigerate. It will keep undamaged for at least a week, and can then be reactivated for another session of baking.

6 This bread can be proved in *bannetons* (proving baskets), or, with no further moulding, on baking sheets. The shape of the *bannetons* will determine whether you have to mould it into long loaves or leave them round. Whichever shape, make sure the *bannetons* are well floured, and prove the loaves bottom upwards as you will be turning them out on to baking sheets, stones or the floor of the oven itself.

7 Leave for a final proof, covered with oiled clingfilm to prevent skinning. If you take a nut of the dough and put it into a storage jar or jug filled with water at room temperature, it will rise to the surface as the yeasts generate gases - just as your loaves are rising in their baskets. When that nut of dough comes to the surface of the water, then your bread is proved and can go into the oven. Proving should take about 1-1 $\frac{1}{2}$ hours. Meanwhile, heat the oven to 230°C/450°F/gas 8.

8 Turn the loaves on to oiled baking sheets, or a baking stone, slash them with a knife: three slashes close together for round loaves, diagonal cuts down the length of longer breads, and bake them for about 35 minutes, spraying them with water three times in the first 5 minutes. If they do not sound hollow after 35 minutes, bake for another 15 minutes at 200°C/400°F/gas 6. Cool on wire racks.

BAGUETTES

The 'French sticks' that masquerade as baguettes or bâtards (the name by which they go in Paris) have for too long made a nonsense of the great reputation of France for good bread. Hard and tasteless flours, mechanical processes and an incredible acceleration of the old-fashioned steady fermentation are largely to blame. What you get nowadays is little more than crust and air, with no flavour and little texture.

It is possible to recreate something of the beauty of this everyday, sometimes twice a day, loaf of city dwellers throughout France in your own kitchen. True, the crackle and thinness of the crust is easier to achieve if you have a purpose-built baker's oven, but the slightly chewy texture of the crumb, and the lightness of the well-proved dough is quite within the grasp of anyone.

These loaves are made with yeast rather than a leaven, but the fermentation is lengthy to give every chance of developing the flavour, and to reduce the amount of yeast needed to give lift. (Remember, the less yeast, generally the better the taste.) The French call the method *fermentation 'sur poolish'*, a reference perhaps to the influence of Viennese and eastern European bakers on Parisian breadmaking during the first half of the 19th century.

If you do not have *bannetons*, you can lay the loaves immediately on a greased baking sheet (crease downwards), and prove them for slightly less time. Or you can buy specially made French baguette tins, which are economical of space. Equally, you can make what the French call a couche, by flouring a linen cloth and laying each loaf between a fold. Be warned that the knack of extracting the loaves from this arrangement and transferring them to the oven is something learnt in time. Disasters are not infrequent.

How the baguettes are baked will determine the character of the crust. Domestic ovens are often not hot enough, nor do they retain enough humidity to give that defined crackle. It is not satisfactory to bake on more than one level, the lower loaves will not be as good, and changing them round halfway through is not entirely successful. So, if your oven is not large enough to take all the loaves at once you can freeze two of the moulded loaves before they have started their final proof. Take them out the next day and carry on from that point.

Makes four 30 cm / 12 inch loaves
* *300 g / 10 oz unbleached white bread flour*
* *600 ml / 20 fl oz tepid water*
* *15 g / 1/2 oz fresh yeast*
* *2 teaspoons salt*
* *600 g / 1 1/4 lb unbleached white plain flour*

1 In a large bowl, mix the white bread flour with 400 ml/ 14 fl oz of the water, the crumbled yeast and the salt. Beat well with a wooden spoon. Cover and leave to rise at room temperature for about 4 hours, until tripled in size. Add the rest of the water, then the plain flour handful by handful, beating with your hand to stretch the gluten. Once brought together into a softish dough, turn out on to a floured work surface and knead for 10 minutes.

2 Leave the dough to rise in a bowl covered with oiled clingfilm in a warm place (26°C/80°F) for about 2 hours, until at least doubled in size. Return the dough to the lightly floured work surface, divide into four pieces and mould into balls. Leave them to rest for 5 minutes, crease or join side downwards.

3 Take each ball in turn, flip the smooth side underneath and flatten with the palm of the hand. Fold inwards the right and left sides to meet in the centre, and press to secure contact. Each ball will now resemble an oblong cushion. Let them rest at the side of the table. These rests are necessary to ensure that you do not tear the dough while shaping it. The more it is worked, the stronger is its elasticity. When relaxed, it will form the shape you want very much more easily.

4 Take each cushion in turn and lay it smooth side down in front of you, the short sides to the right and left. Roll it back towards you, pressing down with your thumbs the whole length of the fold so as to make firm contact. The first roll completed, pinch the join together between finger and thumb. Leave to rest for 4 or 5 minutes, join uppermost.

5 Roll these squat sausages to and fro with your fingers splayed out across them. Gently tease more length out of them. Do not press or stretch too much. If you encounter resistance, leave well alone, and turn to another loaf. Eventually, you will achieve long loaves of 30 cm/12 inches, with a smooth side unblemished by crease or tear. Flour your *bannetons* (proving baskets) and lay in each loaf smooth side downwards. Cover the tops with oiled clingfilm and leave for the final proof at 26°C/80°F for about 1½ hours. The tops should not spring back when you press them with a floured fingertip. Meanwhile, heat the oven as hot as possible, at least 230°C/450°F/gas 8.

6 When the proof is complete, turn the loaves out of the *bannetons* on to a greased baking sheet. Slash each of them with a sharp, preferably serrated, knife four or five times on a sloping diagonal. The depth of the cut will vary. If they are overproved (see page 26), shallow cuts will not damage an already delicate structure; if they seem resilient and underproved, deeper cuts will help the loaf expand in the oven. Put the loaves on the upper shelf, and spray them with water immediately, using a garden atomizer or the spray attachment from some household cleaner (scrubbed and purified!). After 2 minutes, spray again, and a third time after 5 minutes. Bake for about 20 minutes. The loaves will sound hollow when tapped.

7 If you follow this recipe, each of these loaves will weigh 400 g/14 oz before going into the oven. When they are cooked, they should lose about 12 per cent of their moisture, and will weigh 350 g/12 oz. This is a useful check on whether a loaf is cooked or not. Cool them on wire racks.

Top: When the loaves have proved, turn them out of the bannetons *(proving baskets) on to a greased baking sheet.*

Bottom: Slash each loaf with a sharp, preferably serrated, knife four or five times on a sloping diagonal.

WALNUT BREAD

Pain aux noix

Some people might claim that the most important nut to breadmaking is the chestnut: it was once the staple for many people living in south-western France and was itself turned into flour for making a sort of bread. It still is called le pain de bois - bread of the woods.

The walnut may never have been turned into a loaf, but it has ornamented many, for its rich and seasoned flavour seems to complement the taste of grains - be they wheat or rye. And walnut bread, sometimes sweetened, as here, with raisins or sultanas, is a perfect foil for strong cheese.

This wholemeal loaf is enriched with egg and milk, as well as the filling of nuts and dried fruit. The dough should be quite moist; wholemeal has a tendency to dry out. Remember, too, that wholemeal performs best if it kept warm through the whole process, from mixing to final proof.

Makes 2 round loaves
* 450 g / 1 lb wholemeal bread flour
* 1 teaspoon salt
* 30 g / 1 oz fresh yeast
* 225 ml / 8 fl oz milk at 43°C / 110°F
* 1 egg
* 120 g / 4 oz chopped walnuts
* 60 g / 2 oz raisins or sultanas, warmed slightly
* 1 egg mixed with 2 tablespoons of milk for glaze

Top: *French Hearth Bread.*
Bottom: *Walnut Bread.*

1 In a warmed large mixing bowl, combine the flour and salt. Make a well in the centre and crumble the yeast into it. Pour on the warmed milk and mix with your finger to dissolve the yeast and incorporate a little flour. Whisk the egg and add to the liquid. Sweep with your hand round and round the bowl to progressively incorporate all the dry flour, then mix to a dough. When it leaves the sides of the bowl, turn on to a floured work surface and knead for 8 minutes.

2 Flatten the dough on the work surface and scatter the nuts and fruit over the dough. Press them into it with your fingers, then fold the dough up and place in a bowl. Cover with oiled clingfilm and leave to rise in a warm place (26°C / 80°F) for about 1 1/2 hours, until doubled in size.

3 Turn out the dough on to the lightly floured work surface, knock back lightly and divide in two. Gently mould each piece into a ball. Place on warmed, oiled baking trays and cover with oiled clingfilm to guard against skinning. Leave to prove, well out of any draughts, at between 26°C / 80°F and 29°C / 85°F. Meanwhile, heat the oven to 220°C / 425°F / gas 7.

4 When the loaves are ready (they should no longer spring back when you prod them with a floured finger), brush them both with the glaze and bake for about 35 minutes, exchanging the top loaf for the one at the bottom of the oven halfway through the cooking time. Cool on wire racks.

FRENCH HEARTH BREAD

Fougasse

Fougasses, which can also be called fouacés, are derived from the same Latin word focus, meaning hearth, as the Italian focaccia. They are all hearth breads, baked on the floor of the oven just after the fire has been raked out - when its temperature is too high to bake breads without burning the crust. The baker, anxious to test the temperature, tries a little something; the small child, waiting eagerly for the first pull at fresh bread, has a titbit to quell the pangs of anticipation.

To give some character to the flavour, this bread is fermented on a starter of ripened dough from the previous day's bread-making (it does not have to be fougasse).

Makes 2 loaves
* *225 g/8 oz of the previous day's dough*
* *7 g/^{1}/4 oz fresh yeast*
* *250 ml/9 fl oz tepid water*
* *425 g/15 oz unbleached white bread flour*
* *1 teaspoon salt*
* *1 egg mixed with 2 tablespoons of milk for glaze*

1 Place the previous day's dough in a mixing bowl, crumble in the yeast and add the water. Squeeze the ripened dough through your fingers to break it up and make a rich soup. Mix the flour with the salt and add to the starter in handfuls, beating vigorously the while. Mix to a dough, then turn out on to a floured work surface and knead for 6 minutes. Leave the dough to rise in a bowl covered with clingfilm in a warm place (26°C/80°F) for about 1 ^{1}/2 hours, until doubled in size.

2 Turn out the dough on to the lightly floured work surface, divide it in half and mould two balls. Flatten each with the palm of your hand and fold the left and right hand sides to the centre, as if folding a business letter in three. Press the crease together with the edge of your hand and you should have an oblong cushion shape. Leave to rest under oiled clingfilm for 10 minutes.

3 Using a rolling pin, and with a little flour to stop sticking, roll the two cushions out to rectangles measuring approximately 25 x 15 cm/10 x 6 inches: between 12 and 6 mm/^{1}/2 and ^{1}/4 inch thick. If there is resistance from the dough to rolling, do not force it, but rest the piece and turn to rolling the other one.

4 Using the blade of a metal dough scraper, or a pastry cutter, cut four diagonal tears in each rectangle, going almost, but not quite, from edge to edge. Then lay each fougasse on a large oiled tray, stretching and pulling so that it fills the tray. It need not be immaculately regular, it is meant to seem improvised.

5 Cover the dough with oiled clingfilm and leave to prove for about 30-40 minutes. Meanwhile, heat the oven to 230°C/450°F/gas 8.

6 Brush the loaves with the glaze and bake them for about 20 minutes, changing the baking sheets from the top to bottom shelf halfway through the cooking time. When they are cooked, the loaves will sound hollow when tapped. Cool them on a wire rack.

Using the blade of a metal dough scraper, or a pastry cutter, cut four diagonal tears in each rectangle, going almost, but not quite, from edge to edge.

FRENCH ROLLS

Pistolets

Professor Calvel, the greatest French teacher of baking this century, regarded pistolets as one of the finest bread recipes in the war-chest of the journeyman baker. Somehow, it had survived the onslaught of mechanization - which changed so much about French, and every other, bread - and craftsmen were still seen hand rolling the little forms, splitting them with a broom handle, or the edge of the hand, and carefully nurturing them into perfect dinner rolls.

Rolls are the fancy side of baking. They are not usually made with wholemeal or coarse flours, and the wheat has to be the best to give them maximum lightness. They are made with a slightly enriched dough: the extract of malt gives zip to the yeast and a burnished bronze crust, and the milk powder gives tenderness of crumb.

Split each ball of dough nearly into two by pressing down with a smooth piece of wood, such as a wooden spoon handle, nearly to the table.

Makes 16 rolls
* *300 ml / 10 fl oz water*
* *1 tablespoon dried milk powder*
* *1 teaspoon malt extract*
* *10 g / $^1/3$ oz fresh yeast*
* *500 g / 1 lb 2 oz unbleached white bread flour (for preference, 100 % American or Canadian)*
* *1 teaspoon salt*
* *rye or rice flour for dusting*

1 Mix the water, milk powder, malt extract and yeast together. Mix the bread flour with the salt in a bowl and make a well in the centre. Pour in the liquid and mix to a dough. Turn on to a floured work surface and knead for 8 minutes. The dough will be moist, keep the work surface floured (but not too much) and your hands clean. Leave the dough to rise in a bowl covered with clingfilm at room temperature (21°C/70°F) for 3 hours. Turn out on to the work surface and knock back. Leave to rise once more for about 1 hour.

2 Return the dough to the work surface and divide it into 16 pieces. Roll these into tight little balls by flattening them with your palm on to the table and describing circles with your hand. Gradually lessen the pressure to make a cup of your palm, fingers and thumb. The dough will turn and lift into a ball. Leave these to rest under a cloth for 5 minutes.

3 Split each of these balls nearly into two by pressing down with a smooth piece of wood (like a large wooden spoon handle) nearly to the table. Dust the tops with rye flour or rice flour to stop the dough sticking to the splitting stick. Split each one in turn, then leave to rest again.

4 Returning to the first roll, pick it up between fingers and thumbs and gently stretch it 2.5-5 cm/1-2 inches along the line of crease. Place the rolls on a warmed, oiled baking sheet. Leave to prove, well covered with oiled clingfilm, at 26°C/80°F, until doubled in size. Meanwhile, heat the oven to 230°C/450°F/gas 8.

5 Bake the rolls on the upper shelf in the oven, spraying water into the oven twice in the first 3 minutes. The rolls should be cooked within 15 minutes. Cool on a wire rack.

PAIN POLKA

This rustic and crusted loaf, so deeply cut before baking that you break off tasty mouthfuls with your fingers rather than cutting tidy slices, is made with a starter of the previous day's dough - in France called simply, *pâte fermentée*. If you are not making bread every day, it will keep for longer in the refrigerator. However, the simplest routine is perhaps to make a straightforward bread on one day and keep back enough fresh dough to make a pain polka the next.

Makes 1 large loaf
* *375 g / 13 oz of the previous day's dough*
* *15 g / ^{1}/$_2$ oz fresh yeast*
* *325 ml / 11 fl oz warm water at 26°C / 80°F*
* *640 g / 1 lb 7 oz unbleached white bread flour*
* *15 g / ^{1}/$_2$ oz salt*

1 Put the previous day's dough in a mixing bowl. Crumble in the yeast and add the water. Press the mixture through your fingers until the dough has broken up into a messy soup with a few lumps. Then stir in the flour and salt, handful by handful, mixing vigorously with your hand all the while to absorb each addition. The mix completed, turn the dough on to a floured work surface and knead well for 8 minutes. Leave the dough to rise in a bowl covered with oiled clingfilm in a warm place (24°C/75°F) for about 2 hours, until doubled in size.

2 Turn out the dough on to the lightly floured work surface and at this point remove 375 g/13 oz of the dough and reserve in the refrigerator for the next pain polka. Knock the dough back and mould it into a single ball. Place it on a warmed, oiled baking sheet, cover the moulded loaf with a piece of oiled clingfilm and leave to prove out of draughts at about 26°C/80°F for about 1 ^{1}/$_2$ hours, until doubled in size.

3 When you judge the bread ready, heat the oven to 230°C/450°F/gas 8. Take the loaf, dust flour over the top and press gently yet firmly with your hands to flatten it to about two fingers thick. Then score it deeply with a sharp blade, or serrated knife, in a criss-cross pattern, slicing to within 12 mm/^{1}/$_2$ inch of the bottom. Leave it to recover for 20 minutes.

4 Bake the loaf for 25-30 minutes, spraying it with water from an atomizer, or something similar, two or three times in the first 5 minutes. Cool on a wire rack.

With a sharp blade, or a serrated knife, score the loaf deeply in a criss-cross pattern, slicing to within 12mm/^{1}/$_2$ inch of the bottom.

FRENCH SPICE BREAD

Pain d'épice

All over northern Europe, people once seemed to make celebration biscuits and cookies of gingerbread at the drop of a festive hat. Each town had its own shape, its own recipe, its trademark.

Gingerbread men are still a happy feature on Dutch, German, and British tables, but not something you expect to see in France where the spiced bread pain d'épice has carried the standard of honeyed sweetness coupled with the bite and zest of spices: always symbols of extravagance and celebration.

It was perhaps a speciality of the north and east of the country; and each city, as elsewhere, had its own particular set of ingredients and favoured combinations.

Some pains d'épice are heavy with chopped candied peel and flaked almonds, but this particular recipe is more even in texture, though the aromas in the kitchen as it cooks are heady and intoxicating.

I have used wholemeal rye flour because the texture seems to gain from a little grittiness.

Makes 1 loaf
* 225 ml/8 fl oz honey
* 225 g/8 oz wholemeal rye flour
* 30 g/1 oz white sugar
* 1/2 teaspoon baking powder
* 1/4 teaspoon bicarbonate of soda
* 30 g/1 oz ground almonds
* 2 bulbs stem ginger
* 2 teaspoons fennel seeds
* 1/2 teaspoon ground cinnamon
* 12 cloves, ground
* the grated zest of half an orange
* the grated zest of half a lemon
* a little milk and sugar boiled to a syrup for glaze

1 Warm and melt the honey by standing the jar in a pan of hot water. Measure it into the rye flour in a bowl and mix together with a wooden spoon. Leave, covered, for 1 hour, for the flour to absorb the liquid.

2 Heat the oven to 180°C/350°F/gas 4. Add the rest of the ingredients, except the glaze, and mix with vigour to ensure everything is spread evenly through the dough. This will be rather sticky, it is the pentosans in the rye flour which always make rye more difficult to handle. Knead the dough on a clean work surface for between 5 and 10 minutes. With rye, it helps if you dip your hands into a bowl of water at intervals during kneading, otherwise you seem to get a thin coating of gluey rye paste over everything.

3 Press this dough into a well greased 1 kg/2 lb loaf tin (or use a non-stick tin). Make sure it gets pushed right into the corners, using wet hands or the dampened blade of a plastic scraper.

4 Bake the loaf on the middle shelf of the oven for about 35 minutes, until a skewer inserted into the centre comes out clean. Cracks may open up the top crust, but these are nothing to worry about. When you have taken it out of the oven, brush the top of the loaf with the glaze and return it to the oven for 1-2 minutes to set the glaze.

5 Let the bread stand in the tin for a few minutes, then invert it on to a wire rack. Pain d'épice keeps very well indeed. Because it is made from rye, it is better for being left a couple of days before cutting into thin slices and buttering for an excellent snack.

Variation: Although rye is the customary grain, it is quite possible to substitute wheat and, in this case, you don't need to wait a couple of days before eating it.

FRENCH SANDWICH BREAD

Pain de mie

Pain de mie - literally crumb-bread, i.e. without crust - was first made to satisfy the demands of tourists from Britain or America who found French loaves too crusty, too rustic and perhaps too tasty. All that was in the early years of this century. Now the French, too, have been convinced of the utility of this loaf: at least for some sandwiches and delicate little canapés. Generally, however, they remain wedded to their baguette.

In the days when bread prices were fixed by government decree and profits were minimal, some bakers begrudged the expensive ingredients such as milk and butter that soften the texture of this loaf and keep it looking white. They used instead grated raw potato.

To keep the crust as thin and soft as possible, this loaf is cooked in a covered pan, just as are Scottish tin loaves and the square English sandwich loaves. Without going to the expense of buying a special tin, simply cover a normal bread tin with an oiled baking sheet and put a 2 kg/4 lb weight on the top to hold it down. Alternatively, if you have a cylindrical steamed pudding tin at the back of your kitchen cupboard you can use that.

Makes 1 loaf

* *450 g/1 lb unbleached white bread flour*
* *$^1/_2$ teaspoon salt*
* *15 g/$^1/_2$ oz fresh yeast*
* *$^1/_2$ teaspoon malt extract*
* *300 ml/10 fl oz warm milk*
* *30 g/1 oz butter*

1 Mix the flour and salt in a bowl and make a well. Crumble in the yeast and add the malt extract and milk. Shave thin slivers of butter on to the well of liquid. Stir with your finger to dissolve the yeast and then gradually mix in the flour. Mix until the dough leaves the sides of the bowl, turn on to a floured work surface and knead for 8 minutes. Leave the dough to rise in a bowl covered with oiled clingfilm

at room temperature (21°C/70°F) for about 2 $^1/_2$ hours, then knock it back and let it rise again for 1 hour.

2 Turn out the dough on to the lightly floured work surface and form a ball. Leave to rest, covered with a cloth, for 5 minutes. Flatten the ball with your hands, then roll into a loaf to fit a long, thin tin (either well greased or non-stick), measuring 10 x 33 x 9 cm/4 x 13 x 3 $^1/_2$ inches.

3 The dough should at this point occupy one-third of the tin. Let it rise, covered with oiled clingfilm to prevent skinning, until it has reached three-quarters of the way up the sides. Meanwhile, heat the oven to 220°C/425°F/gas 7.

4 Put the top cover on and bake immediately for about 20 minutes. Remove the cover and continue baking for 15 minutes. Though the crust will not be hard, it should still sound hollow when tapped. Cool on a wire rack.

Note: If you don't care about square slices of bread, this dough still makes an excellent fine-textured loaf. Brush the top crust with beaten egg and bake as normal.

Top: *French Sandwich Bread.*
Bottom: *French Spice Bread.*

ITALIAN BREADS

When the world was ruled from Rome, Sicily was the granary of the Empire. 'Bread and circuses' kept the people happy, and the emperors made sure it was good wheaten bread, not the barley handed out to slaves and prisoners. Italy's love affair with bread has never ceased, though it faltered in the face of industrialization and mass-produced, characterless loaves. Now, however, regional food is once more fashionable and breadmaking restored to its proper place.

One ingredient probably defines Italian bread to the world at large: olive oil. Though it has no part in the thin loaves of big-city bakeries, it enriches and softens the crumb of focaccia and ciabatta - two of the success stories of Italian baking today.

Italian breads are also valued for their rustic simplicity: the open, chewy texture of the pan pugliese, or the denseness of rye bread from the northern mountains near Bolzano, where wheat was not so easy to come by, or the intensity of flavour achieved by the olive bread from the groves by the Ligurian Sea near Genoa. And who hasn't nibbled on a bread stick, while waiting for their meal? Yet further proof of the country's abilities.

Clockwise from centre: *Focaccia, Italian Bread Sticks, North Italian Rye Bread, Tuscan Saltless Bread, Italian Olive Bread Rolls, Italian Country Bread.*

CIABATTA

Italian slipper bread

One of the great successes of British breadmaking in the last ten years has been the overwhelming acceptance of this Italian loaf! The dough and the method come from the north of Italy, around the city of Como at the edge of the great Alpine lake, though it has perhaps travelled further in mind and technological process than actual miles on the road. What appeals especially to the English is the cakey tenderness that comes from olive oil in the dough and the soft yet flavorous crust.

It is not an easy loaf to make at home. There are perhaps two things which set trade bakeries apart from home production. The first is the nature of the ovens, the second is the willingness and ability of the professional to handle moist and difficult doughs.

Ciabatta is one of the wettest and the temptation to add more flour is almost irresistible, even though that would change the nature of the loaf itself. The dough is kneaded in the bowl rather than on the table, which helps combat the temptation. It is unfortunate that different flours need different amounts of water. No recipe, therefore, can get it exactly right. Another temptation for the home cook is to disbelieve the cookery book.

The flour I use every day is a stoneground organic unbleached white flour of breadmaking quality. It absorbs less water than a finely roller-milled North American hard spring wheat, but rather more than a soft flour suitable for general kitchen purposes.

A ciabatta made according to this recipe may have better flavour than a commercial loaf inasmuch as it uses the Italian yeasted starter, biga, which is ripened for 12 hours or more, to add flavour.

You can also control the quality of olive oil in the dough, trying to find something fresh and fruity to give that added pungency, though this recipe does not rely on oil to the extent of some English interpretations.

Pour the risen dough over the centre of the prepared baking sheet. Tease the dough into an oblong about 30 x 15 cm/12 x 6 inches. Use the edge of a dough scraper to push round the edges, or well floured fingertips to push and tuck the edge.

Makes 1 loaf
* *225 g/8 oz biga (see recipe, page 17)*
* *15 g/^{1}/$_2$ oz fresh yeast*
* *200 ml/7 fl oz warm water*
* *300 g/10 oz unbleached white bread flour*
* *1 teaspoon salt*
* *2 teaspoons dried milk powder*
* *1 tablespoon extra virgin olive oil*

1 Put the biga in a large bowl and crumble in the yeast. Pour in the water and mix to a soup, squeezing the dough through your fingers to break it up. Mix the flour with the salt and the milk powder, then add to the liquid in the bowl handful by handful, mixing vigorously all the while.

2 When you have added all the flour, pour in the olive oil and continue mixing with circular sweeps of the cupped hand, lifting the dough and stretching it at each beat. Without using a machine, you are conditioning the flour and stretching the gluten.

3 Although it will continue impossibly wet, all the time you work it, the flour is absorbing the moisture and taking on more of the character of a normal dough.

4 Eventually change the movement to something more like kneading - bringing the hand round in a sweeping motion, then punching the fist right into the dough. Count on performing at least 1,000 mixing or kneading movements. Pause occasionally, to wipe your brow.

5 Leave the dough to rise in a bowl covered with clingfilm in a warm place (26°C/80°F) for about 2 1/2 hours. It will grow considerably. The consistency of the dough makes it unlikely that you will want to knock it back and shape it on the work surface.

6 The simpler procedure is to prepare a warmed baking sheet with a heavy dusting of flour. Pour the risen dough over the centre of the baking sheet, then tease this rough pile into an oblong shape measuring about 30 x 15 cm/12 x 6 inches. Either use the edge of a dough scraper to push round the edges, or well floured fingertips to push and tuck the edge into shape.

7 Shake flour over the top of the loaf, cover it with oiled clingfilm and leave it to prove at 26°C/80°F for about 45 minutes. It will spread as well as rise. Meanwhile, heat the oven to 230°C/450°F/gas 8.

8 Bake the bread in the centre of the oven for about 20-25 minutes. Cool on a wire rack.

FOCACCIA

Italian hearth bread

Although pizza may be the best-loved product of the Italian baker's oven, it could soon be challenged by the focaccia. Both are hearth breads, originally cooked on the oven floor before the chief event of the day, the baking of the really big loaves. The French version of focaccia, fougasse, is given on page 35.

Focaccia was the baker's hors d'oeuvre. As soon as the fire had been raked out, he popped these inside the door to cook quickly while the temperature of the oven settled, the hot-spots on the roof died down, so that the large loaves, that would be left in for an hour or more, would not be irretrievably burned. (Burned bread is almost a thing of the past today, but it happened as regular as clockwork in the old ovens. Grandfathers will remember that their parents would often ask the baker for an outside loaf - one that had been cooked right at the edge of the oven, where the heat was at its most fierce and the crust correspondingly dark.)

Makes 2 loaves
* *30 g/1 oz fresh yeast*
* *280 ml/9 1/2 fl oz warm water*
* *60 ml/2 fl oz white wine*
* *600 g/1 1/4 lb unbleached white bread flour*
* *2 teaspoons salt*
* *2 tablespoons extra virgin olive oil*
* *sea salt crystals and extra virgin olive oil for the topping*

1 Cream the yeast in the water and the wine. In a large bowl, mix the flour with the salt and make a well in the centre. Pour in the liquid and mix to a dough. Mix vigorously until it comes away cleanly from the sides of the bowl. Add the olive oil and mix to incorporate.

2 Turn out the dough on to a floured work surface and knead for 10 minutes. The dough will be moist so keep the hands clean and use the dough scraper to assist in the handling. Use as little dusting flour as possible while working

the dough. Leave the dough to rise in a bowl covered with oiled clingfilm in a warm place (26°C/80°F) for 1-1 1/2 hours, until at least doubled in size.

3 Turn out on to the lightly floured work surface, divide in half and mould into two balls. Pat them flat and extend them with palms and fingers to discs about 25 cm/10 inches in diameter. If they resist your stretching, then let them rest for a few minutes under a sheet of oiled clingfilm. Put them in well greased pizza tins.

4 Cover them with oiled clingfilm and leave them to prove in a warm place (26°C/80°F) for 30 minutes. Remove the clingfilm and dimple the focaccia with the fingertips, pressing nearly to the bottom of the loaf. Replace the clingfilm and let them recover for up to 2 hours. Meanwhile, heat the oven to 230°C/450°F/gas 8.

5 Scatter crystals of sea salt over the surface of the loaves and drizzle oil into the dimples. Bake for about 20-25 minutes, spraying water into the oven with an atomizer three times in the first 5 minutes. If you have to put the tins on different shelves of the oven, swap them from top to bottom halfway through the cooking time. Cool on wire racks.

Dimple the focaccia with the fingertips of one hand, pressing nearly to the bottom of the loaf.

ITALIAN COUNTRY BREAD

Pan pugliese

This flavorous country bread comes from the heel of Italy, Apulia. It has tenderness from the olive oil, lots of taste from the biga, and a deep crust into the bargain. Were it made by an Italian farmer's wife and taken to the village bakehouse to be cooked, it would be proved in a cloth-lined basket and turned out on to a baker's peel before being slipped on to the floor of the oven. The same technique can be followed at home but manoeuvring this soft loaf on to a peel and slipping it on to a sheet or stone already in the oven is a tricky procedure and many will find it safer to turn it carefully out of the basket on to a warmed and oiled baking sheet. Alternatively, it can be proved directly on the baking sheet. It will spread quite alarmingly, and the final rise will be more subject to draughts and patchy cooling, but the end result is still scrumptious.

Knock back the dough on a lightly floured work surface, then shape it into a ball.

Makes 1 large loaf
* *200 g / 7 oz biga (see recipe, page 17)*
* *300 ml / 10 fl oz tepid water*
* *15 g / 1/2 oz fresh yeast*
* *2 teaspoons salt*
* *2 tablespoons olive oil*
* *500 g / 1 lb 2 oz wheatmeal (85% extraction) bread flour; or equal parts unbleached white and wholemeal (100%) bread flour*

1 Combine the biga, water, yeast and salt in a bowl and mix to dissolve the biga by squeezing it through the fingers of one hand. Add the olive oil, then add the flour a cupful at a time, beating all the while. Mix to a dough that has some resilience, then turn it on to a floured work surface to knead. It will be quite moist, but will come together with working as the flour takes up all the liquid. Knead for 10 minutes. Leave the dough to rise in a bowl covered with oiled clingfilm in a warm place (24°C/75°F) for about 2 hours, until nearly trebled in size.

2 Turn out the dough on to the lightly floured work surface, knock back and shape into a ball. Prove it either upside down in a floured, cloth-lined proving basket or the right way up directly on an oiled and warmed baking sheet. Leave the dough to prove, covered by oiled clingfilm, for about 1-1 1/2 hours, until doubled. Meanwhile, heat the oven to at least 230°C/450°F/gas 8 and put a deep, but empty, baking tray or roasting pan in the bottom.

3 Dust the loaf lightly and score with a chequerboard of slashes or leave it to crack freestyle in the oven. Place it in the oven and pour a little water into the warmed baking tray or roasting pan, taking care it does not bubble and scald you in the steam. If you have proved in a basket, you will need to have a preheated baking sheet in the oven. Turn your loaf on to a baker's peel, then slide it on to the baking sheet.

4 Bake the loaf on an upper shelf in the oven for about 30-40 minutes. If your oven gets really hot, turn it down to 220°C/425°F/gas 7 after 20 minutes to avoid the crust being too browned. The loaf is cooked when it sounds hollow when tapped. Cool on a wire rack.

ITALIAN OLIVE BREAD

Olive bread has become greatly fashionable in countries far away from the olive belt. Perhaps it's because the flavour captures best those hot Mediterranean evenings.

Makes 1 loaf or 6 rolls
* 350 g/12 oz unbleached white bread flour
* ¹/2 teaspoon salt
* 15 g/¹/2 oz fresh yeast
* 150 ml/5 fl oz tepid water
* 2 tablespoons olive oil
* 175 g/6 oz olives (black, or a mixture of black and green)

Left: *Italian Olive Bread Rolls.*
Right: *North Italian Rye*

1 In a bowl, mix the flour and the salt together, make a well in the centre and crumble in the fresh yeast. Pour the water over the yeast and stir with your finger to cream it. Add the olive oil, and extend your stirring in scope and force to incorporate the flour. Mix vigorously, eventually changing the movement of the hand from something akin to stirring to something more like kneading - bringing the hand round in a sweeping motion, then plunging the thumb right through the dough with a sharp punch. Do this about 100 times, then leave the dough to rest, covered, for 15 minutes.

2 Meanwhile, stone and chop the olives. Scatter them over the dough and knead in the bowl to mix them in. Turn the dough on to the work table and knead conventionally to ensure that the olives are evenly distributed. Leave the dough to rise in a bowl covered with oiled clingfilm in a warm place (24°C/75°F) for 1 ¹/2 hours, until doubled in size.

3 Turn out the dough on to the lightly floured work surface, knock back lightly and mould into a single loaf - either a ball or an oval - or individual rolls directly on a warmed, oiled baking sheet. To make an oval, flatten the dough into a round and fold it in half away from you, to make a half-moon and press the two halves together. Start rolling towards you from the centre, pinching the join with the heel of the hands as you make each turn. The roll completed, pinch the crease between finger and thumb. Tidy the points by gently rolling on the table with the palms of your hands.

4 Cover with oiled clingfilm and leave to prove at 26°C/80°F for about 1 ¹/2 hours. Meanwhile, heat the oven to 220°C/425°F/gas 7. Brush the bread with olive oil and make three diagonal slashes on the top if making a loaf. Bake a loaf for 35-40 minutes, rolls for about 15 minutes. Cool on a wire rack.

NORTH ITALIAN RYE BREAD

In the mountains of the north of Italy, wheat is as difficult to grow as it is in other European highlands, and breads of other grains have been a staple for centuries past. Rye is the most important, and in those districts that have belonged to the Austrian and German sphere of influence, for instance the Tirol, their baking forms part of the larger Central European tradition.

I first heard about this rye and wheaten bread from Carol Field's intelligent book about Italian baking, *The Italian Baker*. It is yeast-based, rather than a sourdough, and uses the gluten of wheat flour to make a lighter loaf. It is made with the Italian yeast starter, biga, which has a particularly good flavour due to its long fermentation time.

Makes 1 large loaf

* 175 g/6 oz biga (see recipe, page 17)
* 15 g/¹/2 oz fresh yeast
* 350 ml/12 fl oz warm water
* 450 g/1 lb wholemeal rye flour
* 225 g/8 oz unbleached white plain flour
* 1 tablespoon salt
* 2 teaspoons crushed caraway seeds

1 Put the biga in a bowl and crumble in the yeast. Add the water and mix to a soup by squeezing the biga through your fingers.

2 Mix the flours, salt and caraway seeds and add them to the liquid gradually, mixing all the while. Mix to a dough, then turn out on to a floured work surface and knead for 10 minutes. Add more water if it seems too stiff, or knead it with your hands repeatedly wetted in a bowl of warm water. The rye will make the dough sticky, so keep your hands and work surface clean.

3 Leave the dough to rise in a bowl covered with oiled clingfilm in a warm place (29°C/85°F) for about 2 hours, until doubled in size.

4 Turn out on to the lightly floured work surface. Knock back and mould into a ball. Flatten this to a disc under the weight of your hand, then fold the right and left sides in to meet at the centre. Roll this cushion shape into a long roll, pinching the join between finger and thumb.

5 Either put this roll into a floured proving basket, seam uppermost, for the final proof, or place it seam downwards on a greased and warmed baking sheet. Cover with oiled clingfilm and leave to prove in a warm place (29°C/85°F) for about 1-1 ¹/2 hours. Meanwhile, heat the oven to 230°C/450°F/gas 8.

6 Make four or five holes down the centre line with a skewer to enable the loaf to expand. If you have proved in a basket, you will need to have a preheated baking sheet in the oven. Turn your loaf on to a baker's peel, then slide it on to the baking sheet and make the holes.

7 Bake for 20 minutes, spraying water on to the loaf three times in the first 5 minutes. Then reduce the heat to 200°C/400°F/gas 6 and bake for another 20-30 minutes, until the loaf sounds hollow when tapped. Cool on a wire rack.

TUSCAN SALTLESS BREAD

One of the paradoxes of recipes for this deservedly popular bread is that many of them suggest adding a pinch of salt to make it more palatable. Bread without any salt is strangely mute, though when this commodity was hard to come by or heavily taxed, it was often omitted by bakers. The French once used to think English bread impossibly salty, high seasoning masking the natural nuttiness of the flour.

Salt does have a useful function, particularly in yeasted breads. Although salt may attack yeasts, even kill them if used to excess, it conditions the flour, makes it firmer and more resilient, while yeast in a way makes flour softer and less textured.

To make the starter, pour the boiling water on to the flour and mix to a batter. Leave overnight.

The saltless bread of Tuscany gets round the problem of flavour by being a natural accompaniment to salty foods like cured hams, salamis, or anchovies. Its open texture and rustic character ensures that it looks the part as well as tastes it.

You need to make the starter for this bread the day before you bake it.

Makes 1 loaf

Starter
* 200 ml / 7 fl oz boiling water
* 120 g / 4 oz unbleached white bread flour

Dough
* 175 ml / 6 fl oz warm water
* 15 g / 1 1/2 oz fresh yeast
* 450 g / 1 lb unbleached white bread flour

1 To make the starter, pour the boiling water on to the flour and mix to a batter. Leave overnight.

2 The next day, add the warm water to the starter and crumble in the yeast. Mix to a soup. Add the flour and mix or knead in the bowl to quite a slack dough. Knead carefully for 5 minutes, keeping your hands as clean as possible. Leave the dough to rise in the bowl covered with oiled clingfilm in a warm place (26°C/80°F) until doubled in size.

3 Turn out on to the well floured work surface and lightly fold the dough into a ball. Place this on a 30 cm/12 inch square baking tray liberally scattered with flour, with the crease or joins uppermost. Cover with oiled clingfilm and leave to prove until again doubled in size.

4 Have ready a similar baking tray, oiled and slightly warmed, place it carefully on the top of the risen loaf so that the shape is somewhat flattened then flip it over when the smooth and floury side will be facing upwards. Let it recover for 20 minutes. Meanwhile, heat the oven to 220°C/425°F/gas 7.

5 Either slash the top with a sharp serrated knife, or leave it to crack freestyle in the oven. Bake for about 35 minutes, until golden. Cool on a wire rack.

ITALIAN BREAD STICKS

Grissini

Home-made grissini put to shame any manufactured ones. They have taste for one. Eating them reminds us what a good idea they are as a plaything for the hands and mouth before a meal: 'they make so pleasant a noise between the teeth,' was the comment of one 19th century novelist on discovering them in Piedmont, their original north Italian home.

Makes 15 sticks

* *15 g/¹/₂ oz fresh yeast*
* *250 ml/9 fl oz tepid water*
* *450 g/1 lb unbleached white bread flour*
* *2 teaspoons salt*
* *3 tablespoons olive oil*
* *sesame seeds or poppy seeds for topping (optional)*

1 Cream the yeast in the water. In a large bowl, mix the flour with the salt. Make a well in the centre, pour in the yeast mixture, then the olive oil. Mix to bring the dough together, then turn out on a floured work surface and knead for about 10 minutes. It is a soft dough.

2 On a floured board, shape the dough into an oblong cushion or rectangle about 30 x 10 cm/12 x 4 inches. Cover with oiled clingfilm and leave to rise in a warm place (29°C/85°F) for about 1 ¹/₂ hours, until doubled in size. Meanwhile, heat the oven to 200°C/400°F/gas 6.

3 When the dough is fully risen, either simply leave plain, or brush lightly with water and sprinkle generously with sesame or poppy seeds. Cut the oblong crosswise into three sections, then cut one section into five and lift and stretch each piece until it becomes a stick. They will not need rolling, but the dough is soft enough to stretch virtually under its own weight. Lay the sticks on a slightly warmed and greased baking sheet. Repeat with the two other sections.

4 Bake for 15-20 minutes, changing the baking sheets from top to bottom halfway through the cooking time if you have had to use more than one. Cool on a wire rack.

Variation: The action of the dough can be accelerated by the addition of a teaspoon of extract of malt at the first mix. This dough makes an excellently light tin loaf, tender to the tongue, with the crispest of thin crusts. Don't cut it into breadsticks, but mould it for a tin, prove for 40 minutes, then brush the top with beaten egg and milk to glaze, and bake in a hot oven.

Above: *Lift and stretch each piece of the dough until it becomes a stick. Lay the sticks on a warmed and greased baking sheet.*

BRITISH BREADS

There is more to British bread than sometimes appears. Not everything is factory-produced, bland and spongy. When it really did seem as if the British were to suffer just that fate, people began to appreciate that different recipes, and more complex procedures, could produce bread worth eating again. Valuable lessons have been drawn from bakers around the world that methods need to change as well as appearance.

Britain has favoured yeast as the powerhouse of its bread for many centuries: it must be all that beer we drink. Sourdough leavens have existed, but not survived. In earlier times, care was taken to keep the amount of yeast to a minimum, and work to long fermentation times which enhanced the flavour of fairly straightforward doughs. But this too has largely gone by the board in favour of highly yeasted short-process breads.

What struck foreign visitors to Britain most forcibly in historical times was the affection for white bread shared by all sections of the population, rich or poor. Though highland regions might have been forced to eat rye, barley or oats cooked on a griddle rather than in ovens, the great bulk of the nation ate fine (or not so fine) white loaves. It is a modern paradox that brown flour, despised for centuries, has become a premium food in the search for better health.

Clockwise from centre: *English Wholemeal Bread, Harvest Loaf, Saffron Bread, Cottage Loaf, Barley Bannock, Split Tin Loaves and Soda Bread.*

BARLEY BANNOCK

Bannock is a generic description of flat breads cooked in Scotland, Ireland and the north of England - i.e. all those regions where wheat was not the primary staple grain. The grain used in bannocks might differ, just as it does in loaves of bread, but the common factor was that they were cooked on a griddle and were unleavened.

They are very delicious. Not as enriched as girdle or drop scones, certainly not as sweet, but they make a wonderful tea bread nonetheless. In this recipe, the bannock is cut into sections before being cooked. Strictly speaking, once they are cut, they are 'scones', though common usage would now have it that scones are sweetened and have currants in them.

Makes 1 round, cut into 4
* *120 g / 4 oz barley flour*
* *60 g / 2 oz unbleached white plain flour*
* *$^1/_2$ teaspoon cream of tartar*
* *$^1/_2$ teaspoon salt*
* *150 ml / 5 fl oz milk and plain yoghurt mixed half and half, or buttermilk if available*
* *$^1/_2$ teaspoon bicarbonate of soda*

Above: Form the dough into a ball and press it with your hand to form a disc about 12mm/$^1/_2$ inch thick. Cut the disc into four.

Right: Cook the bannock sections on a preheated griddle for 4-5 minutes on either side until brown.

1 Sift the flours, cream of tartar and salt together into a bowl. Mix the milk and yoghurt with the bicarbonate of soda and add to the bowl. Bring together into a soft dough, which you may work briefly on a floured work surface. Form the dough into a ball and press it with your hand to form a disc about 12 mm / $^1/_2$ inch thick. Cut the disc into four.

2 Heat a griddle on the top of the stove (if you don't own a griddle, use a heavy frying pan). It should be hot but not burning - feel the heat with your hand about 2.5 cm / 1 inch above the surface, it should warm the palm.

3 Cook the bread for 4-5 minutes on either side until brown. Wrap them in a cloth to keep the outsides soft and eat them quite quickly after cooking.

SPLIT TIN LOAF

Although many British loaves, especially in the last 30 years, have become simple doughs that take no more than an hour or two to make, there are more lengthy processes that still find favour particularly because they allow time for the wheaty taste to develop, and for as little yeast as possible to be used - both economical and good for long-keeping.

One of those methods is called the Scottish sponge, because a runny sponge was made the night before which acted as a ferment for the whole dough. These loaves are made according to that system. They are baked together in a block, though not in the same tin. You will find that packing them close together in the oven encourages high rise, and sometimes a wild movement towards each other.

Makes 4 loaves

The first sponge
* 450 g/1 lb unbleached white bread flour
* 1 teaspoon salt
* 7 g/¹/4 oz fresh yeast
* 250 ml/9 fl oz cold water

Second stage
* 800 ml/27 fl oz tepid water
* 4 g/¹/8 oz fresh yeast
* 700 g/1 ¹/2 lb unbleached white plain flour
* 15 g/¹/2 oz salt

Final dough
* 800 g/1 ³/4 lb unbleached white plain flour
* 37 g/1 ¹/4 oz salt
* 60 ml/2 fl oz tepid water

1 Mix the flour for the first sponge with the salt in a medium-sized bowl. Make a well in the centre and crumble in the 7 g/¹/4 oz yeast. Pour the cold water over the yeast and stir with your finger to dissolve. Draw in the flour and mix thoroughly. Turn out on to a floured work surface and knead for 10 minutes, until entirely smooth. It will be a firm dough. Leave the dough to rise in a bowl covered with oiled clingfilm at room temperature overnight.

2 The next day, break the ball of risen sponge into small pieces in a larger bowl, sufficient to take the final dough. Pour on the tepid water for the second stage and mix to a slurry, squeezing it through your fingers. Crumble the 4 g/¹/8 oz yeast into this thick soup, then add the flour and salt for this stage, mixing vigorously. At this stage the dough will be very moist and impossible to knead. Give it at least 200 beats with your hand, or a large mixing spoon, to condition the flour. Leave the bowl covered with oiled clingfilm in a warm spot for about 1 hour, when it should have doubled.

3 Mix together the flour and salt for the final dough, then mix it gradually into the sponge. When all of it has been added, bring in the last stragglers of dry flour with a little tepid water. Mix until it leaves the sides of the bowl. Turn on to the floured work surface and knead for 10 minutes. The dough will be supple, but not too wet.

4 Leave it to rise in a bowl covered with oiled clingfilm in a warm place for about 1 ¹/2 hours until doubled in size. Turn out on to the lightly floured work surface, divide into four and form into balls. Roll into shape and place in four warmed and greased 1 kg/2 lb bread tins. Cover with oiled clingfilm and leave to prove in a warm place until domed above the tops of the tins. Cut the loaves with a sharp knife down the length of the top to give a 'split tin' shape, if wished. Meanwhile, heat the oven to 230°C/450°F/gas 8.

5 Bake the loaves close together at the top of the oven for 15-20 minutes, then reduce the oven temperature to 200°C/400°F/gas 6 and bake for another 20 minutes. Cool the loaves on wire racks.

ENGLISH WHOLEMEAL BREAD

The English were a nation of white bread enthusiasts. Foreign visitors remarked how even the poorest classes afforded white bread, made from flour bleached by most dubious methods. Brown bread, as in ancient Rome, was thought the diet of failures and criminals. How this has changed since we discovered the benefits of bran, and since we found that much mass-produced white bread was devoid of texture or flavour.

Makes 2 loaves

* 800 g/1 ³/4 lb stoneground wholemeal bread flour
* 15 g/¹/2 oz salt
* 25 g/³/4 oz fresh yeast
* 475 ml/17 fl oz warm water (38°C/100°F)
* 60 ml/2 fl oz vegetable oil

1 Preheat the oven to its minimum temperature. Warm the mixing bowl under hot running water, put in the flour and salt and warm in the cool oven until blood heat. Make a well in the middle and crumble the yeast into it. Pour on a third of the water and stir with a finger. Leave for 3 minutes, then add the rest of the water and the vegetable oil.

2 Mix the flour into the liquid. Continue to mix until you have a shaggy mass with the flour evenly wetted. Turn out the dough on to a floured work surface and knead until it comes away cleanly from the surface and shows considerable elasticity - this can take anything from 8-15 minutes. Replace the dough in the bowl. Cover it with oiled clingfilm. Leave it to rise in a warm place (26°C/80°F) until doubled in size.

3 Turn out the dough on to the lightly floured work surface and knock it back. Divide into two and shape gently into two balls. Leave to rest for 3 minutes while you warm and grease two 1 kg/2 lb loaf tins, measuring 11 x 22 x 6 cm/ 4 ¹/2 x 8 ¹/2 x 2 ¹/2 inches, or one 2 kg/4 lb tin, measuring 13 x 30 x 10 cm/5 ¹/2 x 12 x 4 inches. Shape the loaves by flattening lightly and rolling into a stubby sausage, and put

them into the tins. If using one large tin, mould the loaves as two balls and place them next to each other. They will part easily. Cover with oiled clingfilm and leave to prove in a warm place (26°C/80°F) until they rise to the top of the tins. Meanwhile, heat the oven to 230°C/450°F/gas 8.

4 Place the bread on an upper middle shelf and bake for 15 minutes, spraying the oven with water twice in the first 5 minutes. Then reduce the oven temperature to 200°C/400°F/gas 6 and bake for another 15 minutes. Test the loaves to see if they are cooked. They will sound hollow when tapped. If the crust is not sufficiently crisp when the loaves are cooked, return them to the oven, without their tins, for another 10 minutes. Cool on wire racks.

Top: *English Wholemeal Bread*
Bottom: *Saffron Bread*

SAFFRON BREAD

This recipe is by now traditionally connected to the county of Cornwall, but it was not always so. The crocuses whose stamens are saffron were cultivated throughout southern England, just as they were in continental Europe and further afield. Medieval cooks loved the golden colour, as well as the heady flavour. By the Victorian period, however, Cornwall and the south west were particular strongholds of the taste. They called it 'cake' rather than bread, but it was cooked as bread or buns, not generally as a round cutting cake.

Makes 2 loaves

Saffron infusion
* 1 g (1 packet) saffron stamens
* 90 ml / 3 fl oz water
* 1/2 teaspoon white sugar

First stage
* the saffron infusion
* 200 ml / 7 fl oz tepid milk
* 1/2 teaspoon white sugar
* 25 g / 3/4 oz fresh yeast
* 60 g / 2 oz unbleached white bread flour

Second stage
* 400 g / 14 oz unbleached white bread flour
* 1/2 teaspoon salt
* 60 g / 2 oz white sugar
* 60 g / 2 oz butter
* 1 large egg
* 1 teaspoon lemon juice
* the ferment made in the first stage
* 120 g / 4 oz sultanas, slightly warmed

Glaze
* 60 g / 2 oz white sugar
* 30 ml / 1 fl oz water
* squeeze of lemon juice

1 To make the saffron infusion, empty the saffron into the water in a pan and bring to the boil. Add the sugar and let steep off the heat for 30 minutes. Bring to the boil again and cool to tepid. Mix the saffron infusion with the tepid milk and the 1/2 teaspoon sugar. Crumble in the yeast and stir in the flour for the first stage. Leave to ferment for 30 minutes.

2 Put the flour, salt and sugar for the second stage in a bowl and rub in the butter. Mix the egg and lemon juice into the ferment. Make a well in the centre of the flour and pour on the liquid. Mix to a dough. Turn on to a floured work surface and knead for 5 minutes. The dough will be soft, try to work it with as little additional flour as possible. Leave it to rest for 15 minutes. Add the warmed sultanas and knead again to incorporate them thoroughly. Return it to the mixing bowl, cover tightly with oiled clingfilm and leave to rise in a warm place (26°C/80°F) for at least 1 1/2 hours.

3 Grease two 1 kg/2lb loaf tins, which should be slightly warmed. Turn out the dough on to the lightly floured work surface, knock back lightly and divide in half. Mould two loaves to fit the tins, cover them with oiled clingfilm and leave to prove in a warm place for about 45 minutes. They should rise to fill the tins. Meanwhile, heat the oven to 220°C/425°F/gas 7.

4 Bake the loaves in the centre of the oven for about 25 minutes. The crust will at first be soft, but they should still sound hollow and feel light when handled. Meanwhile, make the glaze. Put the sugar, water and lemon juice in a pan and bring to the boil. Brush the cooked loaves with the glaze and leave to cool on wire racks.

Note: This bread dries out quite quickly and is best eaten fresh. It can also be toasted, and it makes the basis of a very sophisticated trifle. It is also possible to shape up the dough as buns (to make 12-16). You can make hot cross or any other bun; just omit the saffron and vary the fruit.

COTTAGE LOAF

Place the smaller ball on top of the larger, making sure you position it in the centre, then carefully press a hole through the centre from top to bottom, using the first three fingers and thumb of one hand gathered into a cone shape.

The cottage loaf is perhaps the ultimate symbol of British traditional baking. Yet this shape is one of the most difficult to get right. The dough needs be firm so that the bottom half does not collapse under the weight of the top. The joining of the two needs to be firm yet gentle. All too often, the 'hat' topples off: if it does, console yourself that the bread will be none the worse for being misshapen.

Makes 1 loaf
* 300 g/10 oz unbleached white plain flour
* 150 g/5 oz unbleached white bread flour
* 2 teaspoons salt
* 25 g/^{3}/4 oz fresh yeast
* 200 ml/7 fl oz warm water (26°C/80°F)
* 2 teaspoons vegetable oil
* beaten egg for glaze

1 Sift the flours and salt into a bowl and make a well in the centre. Crumble the yeast into the well and pour on the water. Stir with a finger to dissolve the yeast. Add the oil and mix the dough. When it leaves the sides of the bowl, turn it on to a floured work surface and knead for 10 minutes. The dough will be firm.

2 Leave the dough to rise in a bowl covered with oiled clingfilm in a warm place (26°C/80°F) for 1 ^{1}/2 hours, until doubled in size. Turn out on to the lightly floured work surface, knock back and form two balls, the first of one-third of the dough, the second, two-thirds. Divide by weight if you are unsure. Leave them to rest for 5 minutes, covered with oiled clingfilm.

3 Gently flatten the top of the larger ball and the bottom of the smaller one. Moisten the bottom surface of the smaller one with a brush dipped in water. Place the smaller ball on top of the larger, making sure you position it in the centre, then carefully press a hole through the centre from

top to bottom, using the first three fingers and thumb of one hand gathered into an approximate cone shape.

4 Place the loaf on a floured baking sheet and brush with the beaten egg. Cover with oiled clingfilm as well as a large glass bowl inverted over the loaf, to avoid a skin forming on the outside of the dough. Leave to recover and prove in a warm place (26°C/80°F) for about 40 minutes. Meanwhile, heat the oven to 200°C/400°F/gas 6.

5 When proved, brush again with beaten egg, then, with a pair of scissors, snip small cuts at 5 cm/2 inch intervals round the outsides of both the top and bottom sections of the loaf. These will help the expansion of the loaf in the oven.

6 Bake the loaf in the bottom of the oven, preferably under a 'bonnet' of a large saucepan or metal bowl inverted over the loaf (allowing plenty of room for growth). This will equalize the pull of the oven and encourage the loaf to rise straight, as well as keeping the crust soft and expandible for as long as possible. Bake for 20 minutes, then remove the 'bonnet' and bake for a further 15 minutes so that the crust can brown. Cool on a wire rack.

HARVEST LOAF

Bread has always been turned to purposes other than mere sustenance. Just as it is itself a symbol of survival and nourishment, so particular shapes are used to add further layers of meaning: the plaited strands of the Jewish challah recalling the Temple breads, the Greek loaves in the form of a dove at Eastertide, and so on. In England, the most famous modelled loaf is without doubt the harvest sheaf, displayed in church for the Harvest festival. Its apparently complex form is a simple matter of construction, and its message is unambiguous.

Any number of shapes may be constructed out of bread. If they are dried out very slowly (in an oven on pilot light, for instance), they can be preserved without deterioration for a matter of years. It is best if the dough is made stiff, and the loaf should not be underproved when baked, otherwise it runs the risk of rising too much in the oven, so distorting the chosen form.

Using a sharp knife, cut out a button mushroom shape (with a large head and a short stalk) to fit on a greased baking sheet or an upturned baking tray.

Makes 1 loaf
* *800 g / 1 3/4 lb unbleached white bread flour*
* *15 g / 1/2 oz salt*
* *15 g / 1/2 oz fresh yeast*
* *400 ml / 14 fl oz cold water*
* *1 egg mixed with 2 tablespoons milk for glaze*

1 Mix the flour and salt in a bowl. Make a well in the centre and crumble in the yeast. Add the water and mix with your finger to cream the yeast. Mix in the flour to make a dough. When it leaves the sides of the bowl, turn it on to a floured work surface and knead thoroughly for at least 12 minutes, to clear the dough completely. Leave the dough to rise in a bowl covered with oiled clingfilm in a warm place (24°C/75°F) for 1 1/2 hours, or until doubled in size. Turn out on to the work surface, knock back and form into a ball. Cover with oiled clingfilm and leave to rest for 5 minutes.

2 Flatten the ball with the palm of your hand, fold the right and left sides in to meet in the centre, and press the join together with the heel of your hand. It should resemble an oblong cushion in shape. Flour the work surface and roll out the dough to a rectangle approximately 12 mm/1/2 inch thick. It may need to rest for 5 minutes during this rolling, in order not to tear. Cover it with a cloth if it does need to rest, to prevent skinning.

3 Use a sharp knife to cut out a button mushroom shape (with a large head and short stalk) to fit on a greased baking sheet or upturned baking tray 45 x 30 cm/18 x 12 inches. Lift this shape on to the greased sheet or tray and prick it all over with a fork. This is the base of the wheatsheaf. Brush it with cold water to prevent skinning.

4 Divide the dough that was left after making this shape into two pieces, one twice the size of the other. Reserve the smaller portion under oiled clingfilm. Divide the larger piece into five equal sections, then divide each of those into 16. You should have 80 tiny pieces of dough. Working quite quickly, roll each of these between the palms of the hands to make tapered sausages, i.e. the ears of corn. Use a pair of sharp scissors to snip each ear three times down the centre, and once on either side, as in the illustration below.

5 As they are done, press the ears of corn on to the top half of the base, arranging first a row lapping over the top edge, then a second row overlapping the gaps between those in the first, and so on until the top half of the sheaf is filled. If the base shows signs of drying out, brush it again with water.

6 The final piece of dough should be rolled out to a length about equivalent to the stalk of the wheatsheaf base and cut into 20 or 30 thin strips. Roll lightly and stretch these to fit the base to represent stalks. Build up towards the centre to give it depth of modelling. Plait the last three strips and place them across the join of stalks and ears.

7 Brush the whole loaf with the glaze. Leave it to prove out of all draughts, with a sheet of oiled clingfilm lightly over the top. Watch it carefully to make sure it is put in the oven before it over-proves; conversely, do not put it into the oven too soon, or, it will expand wildly, opening up surface cracks. Meanwhile, heat the oven to 220°C/425°F/gas 7.

8 Brush the loaf with glaze again just before putting it in the oven. Bake for about 20 minutes, then reduce the temperature to 190°C/375°F/gas 5 and bake for another 20 minutes. When cooked, it will sound hollow when tapped on the bottom. As long as you glazed it carefully, the crust will be a uniform gold. Cool on a wire rack.

Note: If your oven cannot take this size of wheatsheaf, reduce it to fit, baking any dough left over as a conventional loaf.

Above left: Divide the larger piece of dough from the trimmings into five sections, then divide each of these into 16. Roll each of these between the palms of the hands to make tapered sausages, i.e. the ears of corn. Use a pair of sharp scissors to snip each ear three times down the centre and once on either side.

Above: Roll out the final piece of dough to make 20-30 thin strips. Fit them to the base to represent stalks, building up towards the centre to give depth.

SCOTTISH BAPS

The bap is a Scottish 'morning goods' - something sold by bakers in time for breakfast, elevenses or lunch. The bun is light as air, and the crust yieldingly soft.

Scottish baps are at their best eaten warm straight from the oven, but they can be reheated very successfully - either warm them through in a low oven or split them and toast under the grill.

Baps also make the ideal packed lunch.

Makes 8
* *30 g / 1 oz fresh yeast*
* *350 ml / 12 fl oz tepid milk and water mixed in equal quantities*
* *450 g / 1 lb plain white flour*
* *2 teaspoons salt*
* *extra flour for dusting*

1 Cream the yeast in the warm milk and water. Sift the flour together with the salt into a large bowl and make a well in the centre. Pour the yeast liquid into the well and mix to a slack dough.

2 Knead lightly in the bowl, then cover with oiled clingfilm and leave to rise in a warm place for about 1 hour, until doubled in size.

3 Turn out on to the lightly floured work surface and divide into eight portions. Knead these into balls, cover and leave on one side for a few minutes.

4 Using a floured rolling pin, gently roll the dough balls into 10 cm / 4 inch rounds. Try to make sure that you roll right to the edge of each round so you do not leave any air trapped there.

5 Lay them out on a greased and floured baking sheet, giving them space to rise and expand. Cover with oiled clingfilm and leave them to prove in a warm place for about 30 minutes, until well risen. Meanwhile, heat the oven to 220°C/425°F/gas 7.

6 Brush the top of the baps with milk, then dust generously with flour (Scottish baps are traditionally floury, rather than glazed). Press a floured finger into the centre of each one to equalize the air bubbles and prevent any blistering on the top when they are baked.

7 Bake the baps for 15 minutes, until lightly browned. Dust them with more flour as soon as they come out of the oven and then leave them to cool on a wire rack. Eat as soon as possible.

BARLEY BREAD

The ancient Greeks once thought barley the prince of grains, though by the time of Imperial Rome it was more often the diet of slaves, and in general it has come far behind wheat and rye as the raw material of bread. One problem is that it has no gluten to provide lift and elasticity, so, unless it is combined with another grain, it will make a heavy loaf. In the highlands of Britain and Europe where wheat does not grow easily, barley has nonetheless held an honourable position in the bakehouse, and its use has sometimes spread beyond the uplands when wet summers have occasioned poor wheat harvests.

Some old bread recipes combine both barley and potatoes for an acceptable loaf, but the recipe given here uses barley and wheat flours.

Top: Barley Bread
Bottom: Soda Bread

Makes 1 small loaf
* 15 g/¹/2 oz fresh yeast
* 225 ml/8 fl oz warm water
* 2 tablespoons double cream
* 175 g/6 oz stoneground brown (85% extraction) flour
* 175 g/6 oz barley flour
* 1 teaspoon salt
* a little egg white mixed with a spoonful of cold water
  for glaze

1 Cream the yeast in the warm water and cream. Mix the flours and salt in a bowl and make a well in the centre. Pour the yeast liquid into the well and mix to a dough. Turn on to a floured work surface and knead for 8 minutes.

2 Leave the dough to rise in a bowl covered with oiled clingfilm in a warm place (24°C/75°F) for about 1 ¹/2 hours, until doubled in size. Turn out on to the lightly floured work surface, knock back and mould into a ball. Flatten the ball with the palm of your hand and carefully roll up to form a simple loaf to fit a slightly warmed and greased 450 g/1 lb loaf tin. Try not to tear the surface of the roll when moulding. Cover with oiled clingfilm and leave to prove in a warm place (at least 24°C/75°F) for 1 hour. Meanwhile, heat the oven to 220°C/425°F/gas 7.

3 Brush the loaf with the egg white and water glaze, and bake in the centre of the oven for about 25 minutes. The loaf is cooked when it sounds hollow when tapped. Leave it to cool on a wire rack.

SODA BREAD

While many soda breads are made with soft brown wholemeal flour, a white loaf is a sparkling and handsome addition to the tea table.

This sort of bread was once universal in Ireland, its especial attraction perhaps being that it was economical on fuel and capable of being cooked in an open hearth rather than demanding an elaborate baker's oven and, like other traditional Irish breads, it did not use yeast but bicarbonate of soda and cream of tartar as raising agents. The normal method of baking was in a covered pot in the embers of the fire. The cook would increase the all-round heat by heaping coals on the lid. My suggestion of a 'bonnet' in the oven recreates this arrangement.

If you prefer to make this bread with brown wholemeal flour - perhaps more authentic - it would be best to find a stoneground flour, ideally as fresh as possible from your nearest watermill or windmill, and to use the softest (weakest) flour they have available, as well as the coarsest grind. You may need more liquid in the recipe.

Buttermilk has become quite difficult to find. It is possible to substitute milk and water with some cream of tartar, or you can use plain live yoghurt.

Makes 1 loaf

* 225 g / 8 oz unbleached white plain flour
* 1/4 teaspoon bicarbonate of soda
* 1/4 teaspoon cream of tartar
* 1/4 teaspoon salt
* 15 g / 1/2 oz butter
* 15 g / 1/2 oz white sugar
* 150 ml / 5 fl oz buttermilk, or half milk, half water plus 1/4 teaspoon cream of tartar
* 1 small egg

1 Sift the flour, bicarbonate of soda, cream of tartar and salt together into a bowl. Rub in the butter and sugar. Mix the buttermilk, or milk and water, with the egg and add to the flour. Mix lightly, then turn on to a floured work surface. It will be quite moist.

2 With clean and floured hands, bring this softly into an approximate round. It will never be smooth and neat as it is best if you do not work the flour too much. If you make a firm dough, which you knead, all you do is excite the gluten in the flour, making the dough tough and heavy. Heat the oven to 180°C/350°F/gas 4.

3 Mark a cross with a knife from one side to the other and place the loaf on a greased baking sheet. Cover this with a 'bonnet' - a tin or saucepan that is larger than the loaf - which will equalize the heat in the oven and give maximum lightness while not browning the crust too much. Bake for 30 minutes, then remove the tin or saucepan and bake the loaf for another 15 minutes, until lightly browned.

4 Soda bread is best eaten warm and fresh. When cooling it on a rack after baking, wrap it in a clean tea towel to keep the crust soft.

Remove the tin or saucepan for the last 15 minutes of the baking time to lightly brown the loaf.

EUROPEAN BREADS

The further east and north you travel in Europe, the more important does rye become as the grain of first resort and wheat second. The strong sour flavours of the breads of Germany and eastern Europe complement the taste of rye perfectly.

The current preoccupation with French and Italian baking should not be at the expense of the immense variety of breads available from Germany, Scandinavia, or Austria, not to mention other Eastern European and Balkan countries. Sometimes they are dismissed as 'pumpernickels' but the finest pâtissiers in Europe are probably Austrian, and it was the combination of Viennese knowhow and strong Hungarian wheat that gave us the commonest European bread form, the French stick.

In those parts of the continent where weather was more extreme and conditions of life more testing, the breads reflected the peasants' preoccupation with survival. It is only in towns and cities that people expected to buy bread everyday, in country districts the oven might not be fired from one month to the next. Hence many of the recipes were for breads that could be dried; others were for very long keepers.

Clockwise from centre: *Vienna Bread, Portuguese Corn Bread, Russian Black Bread, Finnish Easter Bread, Swedish Flat Rye Bread, Pretzels, Austrian Gugelhupf.*

PORTUGUESE CORN BREAD

Broa

Although maize is not native to Europe, it was adopted with great enthusiasm by many communities as soon as it was introduced to them by the explorers of the New World. Sometimes it reached them by circuitous routes - not simply off the boat from Panama - so it goes under names like 'Turkey corn', the new consumers thinking it came from the east, not the west.

Maize was especially valuable to those regions where wheat was not the grain of first recourse, where, for instance, rye and barley, or rice, had been adopted either for reasons of climate, or agricultural preference. Thus is it found on the margins: the north-eastern corner of Italy, or in northern Portugal and Galicia, the region of north western Spain around Santiago de Compostela, where the country is washed by Atlantic rain.

Right: Portuguese Corn Bread

Broa is from north Portugal, the Galicians make a corn and barley bread. This broa is a hearty loaf, eat it with soups and stews and other strong-tasting foods. It can be made with finely ground cornmeal, or you can use polenta if something more crunchy is enjoyed. Although some recipes for cornbread suggest you make a porridge of corn and water - as if making polenta - before combining it with yeast and wheat flour, this method is more direct.

Makes 1 giant loaf
* 300 g / 10 oz yellow cornmeal
* 2 teaspoons salt
* 25 g / ³/4 oz fresh yeast
* 175 ml / 6 fl oz tepid milk
* 300 ml / 10 fl oz tepid water
* 2 tablespoons olive oil
* 600 g / 1 ¹/4 lb unbleached white plain flour

1 Mix the cornmeal with the salt. Cream the yeast in the milk and water and add to the cornmeal. Add the olive oil. Beat in the flour gradually until you have a pliable dough.

2 Turn the dough on to a floured work surface and knead it for 5 minutes. Leave it to rise in a bowl covered with oiled clingfilm in a warm place (26°C/80°F) for about 1 ¹/2 hours, until doubled in size.

3 Turn out on to the lightly floured work surface and knock back vigorously. Form it into a large ball.

4 Place the ball join side downwards on an oiled baking tray. Cover the dough with oiled clingfilm and leave it to prove in a warm place for about 1 hour, until it has doubled in size. Meanwhile, heat the oven to 190°C/375°C/gas 5.

5 Bake the loaf for 35-45 minutes, until uniformly brown and sounding hollow when tapped on the bottom. Cool on a wire rack.

MAJORCAN POTATO BUNS

Coca de patatas

The writer Elizabeth Carter describes in her book *Majorcan Food and Cookery* how these light buns for morning coffee or teatime are often made with the pulp of sweet potatoes but may also be done with the ordinary potatoes that we can buy everywhere.

Makes 8
* 225 g/8 oz potatoes
* 15 g/1/2 oz fresh yeast
* 150 ml/5 fl oz tepid milk
* 225 g/8 oz unbleached white bread flour
* 120 g/4 oz white sugar
* 30 g/1 oz lard
* 1 large egg

1 Bake the potatoes in their skins, then peel them, discarding the skins. Mash the potato pulp with a fork.

2 Cream the yeast in the tepid milk. Mix the flour and potato pulp in a bowl with the sugar. Rub in the lard.

3 Make a well in the centre and add the yeast liquid. Add the egg and mix to a dough. Adjust the texture by adding more milk or more flour. Potatoes will vary in their take-up of liquid. The dough should be moist but not unworkable.

4 Turn the dough on to a floured work surface and knead for 5 minutes.

Turn the dough on to a floured work surface and knead for 5 minutes.

5 Leave the dough to rise in a bowl covered with oiled clingfilm in a warm place (24°C/75°F) for about 1 hour, until doubled in size.

6 Turn out on to the lightly floured work surface and divide it into eight pieces. Shape these into round balls and place them well apart on a greased baking sheet. Cover with oiled clingfilm and leave to prove for 30 minutes, until they have again doubled in size. Meanwhile, heat the oven to 400°C/200°F/gas 6.

7 Bake in the oven for about 15 minutes, until the buns are nicely browned. Cool on a wire rack.

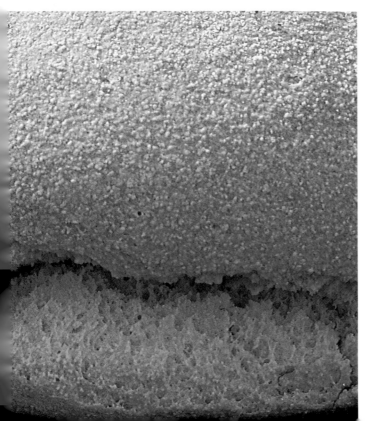

GERMAN SOURDOUGH RYE BREAD

This is a combination bread, using the rising-power of two forms of fermentation: lactic, from the spontaneous fermentation of flour and water with help from wild yeasts - this gives the sour flavour; and alcoholic, from the compressed yeast that we use every day to raise conventional yeasted doughs.

The sourness complements the flavour of rye: one reason for using a sour culture when making rye breads. Rye does not have as much gluten as wheat, hence it benefits from being combined with wheat to make a lighter loaf. There are certain pentosans in rye which make it seem sticky or gluey when being worked. One solution is to knead the dough with wetted hands. The cleaner you keep hands and work surface, the easier kneading will be.

The natural composition of rye flour also means that rye bread is best a day or two old. If you slice it too fresh, the knife glues up and drags across the cut surface. It is wrong to expect rye to make a very airy, light loaf, so slices should be as thin as possible to enhance the bread's tenderness. 'Doorsteps' of rye are all wrong.

I have always followed the advice of my friend Rolf Peter Weichhold, who grinds his own flour in a windmill built on the medieval town walls of Xanten in northern Germany and then bakes it in an oven deep in the fortifications below, that you should start from scratch with this recipe. There is no need to carry over starters or ferments from one batch to the next, although you can set up a routine to do this if you want. This is a three-day recipe, starting from scratch.

Makes 2 large loaves

Days 1-2: the starter
* 60 g / 2 oz stoneground wholemeal rye flour
* 60 ml / 2 fl oz warm water at 43°C / 110°F
* pinch of caraway seeds

Day 3, 9.00 am: the leaven
* 300 ml / 10 fl oz warm water at 43°C / 110°F
* 2 tablespoons of the starter
* 300 g / 10 oz stoneground wholemeal rye flour

Day 3, 5.00 pm: the dough
* 500g / 1 lb 2 oz finely ground wholemeal wheat flour
* 300 g / 10 oz stoneground wholemeal rye flour, plus extra rye flour or rye flakes for rolling
* 15 g / $^1/_2$ oz fresh yeast
* 400 ml / 14 oz warm water at 43°C / 110°F
* 2 teaspoons salt
* the ripe leaven

1 To make the starter, mix the 60 g / 2 oz rye flour and the 60 ml / 2 fl oz water in a bowl, add the caraway seeds and knead with the fingertips to make a dough. Place it in a glass jar and cover with a piece of greaseproof paper. Leave it in a warm place (26°C / 80°F) for 2 days, stirring with a teaspoon twice a day. As it begins to ferment, it will rise and form a domed top. Then the top will flatten, then sink to leave a shallow crater. It is ripe when the top is risen, but flat. It can be refrigerated at this point, and will hold for several days.

The dough for this bread is moulded into two balls and rolled in rye flour or rye flakes before being placed in the tin.

2 On day 3 in the morning, prepare the leaven. Mix the warm water and 2 tablespoons of the starter to a soup. Add the flour handful by handful, mixing all the while. Leave it in a bowl covered with a cloth for about 8 hours, at about 29°C/85°F. When it is ripe, it should taste pleasantly sour.

3 After 8 hours, make the dough. Warm a mixing bowl and warm the flours. Cream the yeast in a small amount of the warm water. Mix the flours and the salt and make a well in the centre, then add the leaven, the creamed yeast and most of the remaining water. Mix to a dough and leave for 10 minutes in a warm spot, covered. Mix again, adding the last of the water, if necessary. The dough should not be too wet. Turn it on to a floured work surface and knead for at least 10 minutes.

4 Leave the dough to rise in a bowl covered with clingfilm in a warm place (29°C/ 85°F) for about 1 ¹/₂ hours, until nearly doubled in size.

5 Turn out on to the lightly floured work surface, knock back and divide into two. Mould the pieces into balls. Grease one 2 kg/4 lb loaf tin, or two 1 kg/2 lb tins. If using a large tin, the balls may be tinned as they are, moistening the tops and rolling them in rye flour or flakes before being placed touching each other in the tin. If using smaller loaf tins, flatten the balls on the work surface, fold the right and left sides of the circle to meet at the centre, turn the shape round so that the long edge faces you and roll up towards you, pinching the join with the heel of hand and thumb as you roll. Moisten the top and roll in rye flour or flakes.

6 Cover the tins with oiled clingfilm and leave to prove for about 30-45 minutes. Meanwhile, heat the oven to 230°C/450°F/gas 8.

7 If baking in the large tin, bake the bread on an upper shelf for 20 minutes, spraying the loaves with water three times in the first 5 minutes. Reduce the oven temperature to 200°C/400°/gas 6 and bake for a further 20 minutes, then reduce the temperature to 180°C/350°F/gas 4 and bake for a final 20 minutes. If using the smaller tins, reduce the 20 minute periods to 15 minutes. The loaves are cooked when they sound hollow if tapped. Cool on a wire rack.

PUMPERNICKEL

Pumpernickel (the Devil's wind, a reference to its causing flatulence) originated in Westphalia on the banks of the Rhine. It is a dark and dense rye bread, cooked extremely slowly, which has no obvious leavening, though it does ferment spontaneously during a long rest in the tin before baking. It is steamed rather than baked, and the slow cooking ensures that it keeps very well. A fact of life is that breads that cook fast are never long keepers, and the giant loaves that once were baked over a matter of hours in a cooling oven would keep for a number of days if not weeks. Pumpernickel, which would keep for months, could be viewed as some form of insurance against a rainy day when the corn ran out and no more bread was to be had - not so unrealistic a possibility when a peasant's life was turned upside down by invasion, pestilence or famine. It was also a way of using the rejects from the corn mill as the best flour for this bread is a really coarse grind, almost a meal. Nowadays, however, it is valued for its intense flavour, a natural foil to foods like smoked hams or strong cheese.

When the cooking is finished, cool it on a rack, and delay slicing the loaf for a day or two, then cut it into the thinnest of slices.

At the beginning of the fermentation time, the dough will come halfway up the tin (see right). By the end of the rising time it will reach the top of the tin.

Makes 2 loaves, or 1 large loaf

* *1.2 litres/2 pints water at 50°C/147°F*
* *1 tablespoon salt*
* *1/2 teaspoon each of ground aniseed, coriander, fennel and caraway*
* *600 g/1 1/4 lb wholemeal rye flour, coarsely ground*
* *450 g/1 lb wholemeal wheat flour, coarsely ground*
* *225 g/8 oz barley flour*
* *15 g/1/2 oz honey (not heat-treated)*

1 Mix all the ingredients, except the honey, in a bowl. Add the honey and continue to mix until it is combined in a dough. Divide between two non-stick baking tins, measuring

11 x 22 x 6 cm/4 1/2 x 8 1/2 x 2 1/2 inches, or one larger tin, measuring 13 x 30 x 10 cm/5 1/2 x 12 x 4 inches.

2 Press the moist dough into the corners and flatten the top with a wetted palette knife. Cover the tin(s) and leave in a warm place (29°C/ 85°F) for 16-20 hours. There will be a spontaneous fermentation and the bread will be seen to rise in the tin. It will also smell quite unusual, but do not be discouraged by this!

3 Heat the oven to 110°C/225°F/gas 1/4 and place a roasting pan of boiling water in the oven and place a rack in the pan. Cover the baking tins tightly with aluminium foil, place them on the rack and bake for 5-6 hours. The loaf should feel firm. Increase the oven temperature to 180°C/350°F/gas 4, remove the foil and bake for another 30-60 minutes to make the top crusty.

4 Leave the bread to stand in the tins for a few minutes, then the loaves should come out easily. Cool completely on a wire rack. Store them wrapped in clingfilm or foil.

PRETZELS

There are two sorts of pretzel (called brezeln in German). One is a hard and salty biscuit that helps sharpen the thirst for a long cool drink of beer, the other is a larger and softer salted bread sold especially in America, having been brought there by German immigrants in the 19th century.

The name refers to the shape, which is very ancient - made by early Christians as a Lenten bread, the crossed arms symbolizing the Cross. The derivation of the name is from the Latin bracellae, 'little arms'. Not only breads, but also sweet biscuits, are made to this pattern in Germany and Austria.

The dough is like a bagel in that it is poached before baking, giving it a chewy texture.

Roll each piece of dough into a pencil, then bend into a horseshoe. Bring the ends up to the top of the shoe, crossing and twisting once in the centre.

Makes 16
* 15 g/¹/2 oz fresh yeast
* 200 ml/7 fl oz tepid water
* 90 ml/3 fl oz tepid milk
* 450 g/1 lb unbleached white bread flour
* 1 teaspoon salt
* 30 g/1 oz butter, melted
* 1 egg beaten with 2 tablespoons milk for glaze
* sea salt crystals

1 Cream the yeast in the water and milk in a bowl. Mix the flour and the 1 teaspoon salt. Make a well in the centre of the flour and pour in the liquid. Mix to a rough dough, adding the melted butter while mixing. Mix thoroughly until the dough leaves the sides of the bowl. Turn on to a well floured work surface and knead for 5 minutes.

2 Leave the dough to rise in a bowl covered with oiled clingfilm in a warm place (24°C/75°F) for about 1 hour, until doubled in size.

3 Turn out the dough on to the lightly floured work surface and knead for another 5 minutes. Divide the dough into 16 pieces. Form them into small balls and leave them covered on the side of the work surface.

4 Ensuring that there is plenty of dusting flour to avoid sticking, roll each piece with the flat of the hands into pencils about 30 cm/12 inches in length. Bend each pretzel into a horseshoe, then bring the ends up to the top of the shoe, crossing and twisting once in the centre. Leave to prove on a floured board, covered with a cloth, for 10 minutes.

5 Heat a large pan of salted water to a bare simmer. Drop each pretzel in turn into the poaching water and remove with a slotted spoon as soon as it rises to the surface. Drain them on a clean tea towel. Meanwhile, heat the oven to 200°C/400°F/gas 6.

6 Place the poached pretzels on greased baking sheets, brush with the glaze and sprinkle them with sea salt crystals. Bake the pretzels for approximately 25-30 minutes, until golden brown. Cool on wire racks.

SWISS PLAITED LOAF

Zopf

People in Switzerland, southern Germany and Austria have a tremendous tradition of fancy baking, for feast days, holidays, or just for Sundays. This plaited bread, ideal for butter and jam for tea or breakfast, but good as well for luxury sandwiches (it contains no sugar), is what the Swiss family likes to eat on a Sunday: home-baked because it is the baker's day off.

There is a symbol behind the plait: it represents the braid of the warrior's widow, cut off before joining him in the afterlife.

Makes 1 loaf
* 600 g/1 ¹/4 lb unbleached white bread flour
* 2 teaspoons salt
* 30 g/1 oz fresh yeast
* 150 ml/5 fl oz milk and 150 ml/5 fl oz soured cream, warmed together to 32°C/90°F
* 1 egg, beaten
* 120 g/4 oz butter, softened
* 1 egg, beaten, for glaze

1 Mix the flour and salt in a bowl and make a well in the centre. Crumble the yeast into the well and add the warm milk and soured cream. Mix to dissolve with your fingers. Add the beaten egg and the butter, and mix to a dough. Turn on to a floured work surface and knead for 5-10 minutes, until soft and shiny. Leave the dough to rise in a bowl covered with oiled clingfilm in a warm place for about 1 hour, until doubled in size.

2 Turn it on to the lightly floured work surface, knock back and form into a ball. Divide this into four and roll each piece into a sausage shape, about 25 cm/10 inches long and 2.5 cm/1 inch thick. With a strong flour, you will have to work in stages, with a little rest between, so as not to stretch the dough too quickly.

3 To make the dough into a plait, press the four long pieces together at one end, giving them a little twist and tuck for neatness.

4 Counting from your left, fold 1 over 2, 3 over 1, 4 under 1, and 4 over 3. Repeat until you reach the end. As you work, the strands will probably lengthen. Nip and tuck the second end in the same way as the first end. Place the finished loaf on a greased baking sheet, cover it with oiled clingfilm and leave to prove in a warm place for about 40 minutes. Meanwhile, heat the oven to 200°C/400°F/gas 6.

5 Brush the loaf with the beaten egg and bake in the centre of the oven for 35-45 minutes. Cool on a wire rack.

Top: To make the plait, press the four long pieces together at one end, giving them a little twist and tuck for neatness.

Bottom: Counting from your left, fold 1 over 2, 3 over 1, 4 under 1, and 4 over 3. Repeat until you reach the end.

VIENNA BREAD

Vienna was in the forefront of European bakery: not just for sweet pastries, chocolate cakes and delicacies like croissants, whose crescent shape was a memento of the defeat of the Turks at the siege of Vienna, but for its bread as well.

Makes 4 loaves

* *30 g / 1 oz fresh yeast*
* *525 ml / 19 fl oz very cold water*
* *900 g / 2 lb unbleached white bread flour*
* *1 tablespoon salt*
* *30 g / 1 oz dried milk powder*
* *30 g / 1 oz butter*

1 Cream the yeast in the water. Mix the flour, salt and dried milk powder in a bowl and rub in the butter. Make a well in the centre and add the liquid. Mix to a dough, which should be moist but not wet. Turn on to a floured work surface and knead energetically for at least 10 minutes.

2 Leave the dough to rise in a bowl covered with oiled clingfilm in a warm place (21°C/70°F) for at least 3 hours. Every hour, knock back the dough in the bowl and replace the cover. This encourages high expansion.

Every hour, knock back the dough in the bowl, then replace the clingfilm.

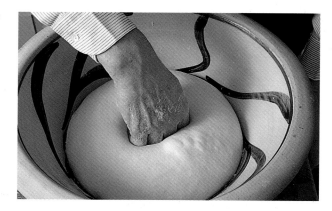

3 When ready for moulding, divide the dough into four pieces and shape them into balls. Leave them to rest, covered and protected from draughts, at the side of the table for 15 minutes. Shape each of them into a baton by flattening the ball of dough with the hand, turning the left and right sides in to meet in the centre, and sealing the joint thus produced.

4 Roll up the oblong cushions by turning with both hands, sealing the joint with the backs of the the thumbs as you roll. After that, extend the length of the loaf by rolling and stretching with the flat of both hands. It is best to make this shape in stages, dealing with each loaf turn and turn about, letting each rest while dealing with the others. This will avoid tearing the dough while stretching it.

5 Once moulded into shape, put them to prove, either seam side downwards directly on greased and warmed baking sheets, or in floured proving baskets seam side uppermost. Cover with oiled clingfilm to avoid skinning. Leave to prove at 29°C/85°F for about 1 hour, or until they have doubled in size. Meanwhile, heat the oven to 230°C/450°F/gas 8.

6 When the loaves are proved, turn them on to warmed and greased baking sheets if you used proving baskets. Slash them four times in slanting diagonals, as if a French stick. Bake on the upper shelf in the oven, creating lots of steam in the oven by spraying water from an atomizer at least three times in the first 5 minutes. Bake for 20 minutes. If you have to bake on two shelves, make sure the trays are swapped over halfway through the cooking time, unless you have a fan-assisted oven. If, at the end of the cooking time, the loaves are not golden-crusted and sounding hollow when tapped, bake for another 10-15 minutes.

AUSTRIAN GUGELHUPF

Kugelhopf

This sweet yeast bread, very similar to the French brioche, is found in a broad belt of Europe, stretching from Alsace (where it is kugelhopf) to Vienna (where they say gugelhupf) and beyond. The word kugel is German for 'ball', and a Jewish round pudding was also called by that name. West or East, the shape is not so much a ball as an inverted decorated bowl with a hole down the middle

Makes 1 large loaf
* 60 g / 2 oz unsalted butter for the mould

The sponge
* 15 g / 1/2 oz fresh yeast
* 120 ml / 4 fl oz tepid milk
* 120 g / 4 oz unbleached white plain flour

The dough
* 120 g / 4 oz unsalted butter
* 90 g / 3 oz sugar
* 2 whole eggs
* 2 egg yolks
* grated rind of 1 lemon
* 1/2 teaspoon salt
* 225 g / 8 oz unbleached white plain flour
* 120 g / 4 oz raisins, plumped in dry white wine

To finish
* icing sugar for dusting

Beat the mixture, lifting and pulling until the dough is workable. Add the raisins and knead to spread them throughout the dough.

1 Chill a large gugulhupf mould in the refrigerator. Melt the 60 g/2 oz butter and let it cool but not set. Brush the inside of the mould all over with the melted butter. Return it to refrigerator to set, then brush again. Keep cool.

2 To make the sponge, cream the yeast in the warm milk, add the 120 g/4 oz flour and mix to make a sponge. Leave in a covered bowl at room temperature overnight.

3 To make the dough, cream the butter and sugar together with a wooden spoon. Add the eggs and yolks, lemon rind and salt, and beat until well combined. Beat in the flour. Add the sponge to this mixture and mix to amalgamate. Beat vigorously with your hand, stretching the dough as much as you can by lifting and pulling. Add a little extra flour to make the dough workable, pulling it away from the sides of the bowl. Give at least 500 strokes. Knead in the raisins.

4 Cover the bowl with oiled clingfilm and leave the dough to rise in a warm place (26°C/80°F) for 1 1/2 hours, or until doubled in size. Turn on to a lightly floured surface, knock back and put in the mould (which it should half fill), cover with oiled clingfilm and leave to prove at 26°C/80°F for about 30 minutes, until it has reached the top of the mould. Meanwhile, heat the oven to 200°C/400°F/gas 6.

5 Bake the bread for approximately 30 minutes before testing with a skewer to see if it is cooked. Insert the skewer into the centre, if it comes out clean, the bread is done. Cooking time will depend on the shape of the mould. Turn out and cool on a wire rack. Dust with icing sugar.

SWEDISH FLAT RYE BREAD

Rågbröd

This bread is quite sensational. Made into a thin sandwich with fresh butter and a sharp yet sweet jam, it is every child's teatime delight. The Swedes make other fragrant rye breads, for instance the limpa, flavoured with orange peel, cumin and other spices. These round flatbreads would keep for a long time, their central holes useful for stringing them together and hanging them to dry in the rafter of the kitchen.

Makes 3 small loaves
* 350 ml/12 fl oz milk
* 30 g/1 oz butter
* 2 tablespoons black treacle or molasses
* 425 g/15 oz wholemeal rye flour
* 15 g/$1/2$ oz fresh yeast
* 150 g/5 oz unbleached white bread flour
* 1 teaspoon salt
* 1 teaspoon ground fennel seeds

1 Warm the milk in a pan and melt the butter in it. Leave until lukewarm (43°C/110°F) and stir in the treacle. Put half the rye flour into a bowl and pour in the liquid. Crumble in the yeast and stir vigorously. Then gradually add the rest of the flours, mixing all time. Finally, add the salt and the ground fennel. Once well mixed, knead briefly in the bowl.

2 Cover the bowl with oiled clingfilm and leave the dough to rise in a warm place (26°C/80°F) for about 3 hours.

3 Turn on to a lightly floured work surface and knead for 5 minutes. The dough will be firm but sticky - one of the facts of life when working with rye flour. Keep your hands clean and moist, and scrape the work surface periodically.

4 Divide the dough in thirds and mould into balls. Flatten these with a rolling pin into 20 cm/8 inch discs. Lay them on a greased baking sheet, prick all over with the tines of a fork and cut a hole in the centre with an egg cup or small pastry cutter. Cover with oiled clingfilm and leave to prove at 26°C/80°F for about 45 minutes, until doubled in size. Meanwhile, heat the oven to 190°C/375°F/gas 5.

5 Bake the loaves for about 25 minutes. When cooked, they will be light brown and sound hollow when tapped. Brush their tops with water and cool on a rack, each loaf wrapped in a clean tea towel to keep the crust soft.

Left: *Finnish Easter Bread*
Right: *Swedish Flat Rye Bread*

FINNISH EASTER BREAD

Country life in Finland can never have been easy: the climate sees to that. Small wonder, therefore, that their breads - which used to be predominantly of rye, barley and oats rather than wheat (and even of root crops and potatoes when the corn ran out) - were often designed for long keeping. There is a wonderful variety to them, kept alive by many self-sufficient and conservative home bakers (towns and villages were too sparse for there to be much professional baking trade), ranging from the unleavened barley and oat breads of the north, the softer rye breads of the eastern regions, to the dried discs.

True to type, festivities occasioned their own special loaves, and this Easter loaf made with yoghurt is baked as a hemisphere, a common festive shape, enriched with sultanas and nuts, and sweetened with a malt glaze. Perhaps to mark the fact it was a high-day, the bread was often a wheat and barley loaf, not everyday rye. As this shape is difficult to provide from implements commonly found on one's pot shelf, I suggest you make it in a well greased 2.4 litre/4 pint saucepan or even a large cake tin, and cut it like a cake.

Makes 1 loaf

The sponge
* 15 g/^{1}/$_2$ oz fresh yeast
* 120 ml/4 fl oz yoghurt
* 120 ml/4 fl oz hot water at 54°C/130°F
* 120 g/4 oz unbleached white bread flour

The dough
* 60 g/2 oz butter
* 2 tablespoons dark brown sugar
* 3 egg yolks
* grated zest of 1 orange
* grated zest of ^{1}/$_2$ lemon
* 1 teaspoon ground cardamom
* 120 g/4 oz barley flour

* 225 g/8 oz unbleached white bread flour
* 1 teaspoon salt
* 3 tablespoons sultanas
* 2 tablespoons slivered almonds
* 3 tablespoons malt extract for glaze

1 To make the sponge, cream the yeast in the yoghurt and water, then mix in the flour, stirring until smooth. Leave to stand, covered, for 2 hours at 24°C/75°F.

2 To make the dough, melt the butter with the brown sugar, cool slightly and, off the heat, add the yolks. Stir this into the sponge together with the zests and spice. Mix the flours and the salt and add gradually to make a dough. Knead well on a floured surface for 10 minutes.

3 Flatten the dough on the table with the palms of your hands and spread the fruit and nuts over the surface. Roll up and knead briefly to spread them throughout the dough. Leave the dough to rise in a bowl covered with oiled clingfilm in a warm place (26°C/80°) for approximately 1 hour, until doubled in size.

4 Turn out on to the lightly floured work surface and knock back. Mould into a ball, then flatten to the approximate diameter of a greased and slightly warmed saucepan or round tin. It should occupy no more than half the container. Cover the top with oiled clingfilm and leave to prove at 26°C/80°F, out of any draught. Meanwhile, heat the oven to 180°C/350°F/gas 4.

5 Bake the loaf for about 1 hour, until a fine skewer inserted into the centre comes out clean. Leave it to rest in the pan for 10-15 minutes before turning on to a wire rack to cool. Melt the malt extract and brush it all over the crust.

RUSSIAN BLACK BREAD

Elena Molokhovets, the Mrs Beeton of Czarist Russia, wrote of making bread on a country estate: of keeping sourdough cultures alive from one baking to the next by the simple procedure of not washing out the wooden troughs in which the dough was mixed; of drying flours in front of the fire before they could be used to make bread; of putting white loaves to prove in a tub of cold water - when the loaves rise to the surface, they are ready for the oven; and of making wheat loaves with skimmed milk or yoghurt, but rye bread with water.

'Black' bread - which was the food of peasants rather than princes - may have been more brown than black, but might contain wheat as well as rye. Its sourness is sweetened by molasses, which also help colour it. This recipe uses toasted breadcrumbs, again it helps the colour, but it also makes a lighter loaf. In Germany it is common practice among professional bakers to recycle stale rye bread in this way.

Mix all the ingredients for the leaven in a bowl and leave in a warm place (24°C/75°F) for 15-24 hours.

Makes 1 loaf

The leaven
* 200 g/7 oz wholemeal rye flour
* 200 ml/7 fl oz warm water
* 2 tablespoons of rye starter (see German Sourdough Rye Bread, page 76)

The dough
* 4 tablespoons molasses
* 250 ml/9 fl oz hot water
* 15 g/¹/₂ oz fresh yeast
* 120 g/4 oz fine rye breadcrumbs, toasted
* ¹/₄ teaspoon ground ginger
* 1 teaspoon ground caraway seeds
* 200 g/7 oz wholemeal rye flour
* 200 g/7 oz wholemeal wheat flour
* 2 teaspoons salt

1 Mix all the ingredients for the leaven together in a bowl and leave in a warm place (24°C/75°F) for 15-24 hours.

2 To make the dough, dissolve the molasses in the hot water, then add the yeast. Add the breadcrumbs and the spices, and mix together. Leave to stand for 30 minutes. Add the leaven, then the flours mixed with the salt. Mix to a dough, then turn out on to a floured work surface and knead for 10 minutes. Do not make the dough too stiff.

3 Leave the dough to rise in a bowl covered with oiled clingfilm in a warm place (24°C/75°F) for 2 hours, until doubled in size. Turn out on to the lightly floured work surface, knock back and mould into a round loaf. Prove on a warmed greased baking sheet, covered with oiled clingfilm, at 26°C/80°F, for about 45 minutes. Do not overprove. Meanwhile, heat the oven to 230°C/450°F/gas 8.

4 Slash the bread with a small cross on the top. Bake for 15 minutes, spraying the oven with water from an atomizer two or three times in the first 5 minutes. Reduce the oven temperature to 200°C/400°F/gas 6 and bake for another 30-45 minutes. The bread is cooked when it sounds hollow when tapped on the bottom. Cool on a wire rack.

AMERICAN BREADS

The United States may be thought a melting-pot of the world's peoples; it is also a bread basket. As each wave of immigrants laps the shore, so they bring their food culture and their breads. Things that have almost lapsed in their place of origin suddenly crop up with greater force and popularity in the USA: think of bagels and pretzels. This makes the breads of America especially interesting.

America became the grain store of the world, once the prairies had been colonized. American spring wheat makes wonderfully light bread, and American baking itself has adopted with enthusiasm the idea of lightness, and combined it with a certain affection for sweetness, so that everyday breads are sometimes thought lacking any character at all. This has been changing in the recent past as young American bakers have been reabsorbing some of the traditional European methods and exploring the creation of longer process breads and loaves with fuller, more bread-like, flavour. There is now a vigorous group of new-wave bakeries offering sourdoughs and traditional breads of great quality, as well as more innovative recipes that combine flavours and ingredients that would never have occurred to earlier tradesmen.

Clockwise from centre: New England Buttermilk Rolls, San Francisco Sourdough, Southern Corn Bread, San Francisco Sourdough, Boston Brown Bread.

SAN FRANCISCO SOURDOUGH

The pioneers who marched west in America, who followed the trail into the prairie vastness, or eagerly set forth to pan for gold in California or the Yukon, were hardly able to rely on bakers and grocery stores for an ounce or two of yeast. They took their own leavening: a smidgeon of dough kept back from the last baking which could be reactivated for the next. If it was stored deep inside a sack of flour, it was proof against frosts, heatwaves, even Indian attacks!

So it was that they were called 'sourdoughs', but it was only those who got as far as San Francisco who were to be able to make this very specific sourdough, which develops its tang from the particular bacilli that seem partial to the air in the Bay. Everyone's air is different, so a true San Francisco sourdough may be impossible to repeat elsewhere, as the leaven will take on different microbes and wild yeasts, depending on the kitchen, bakery and climate.

If you have no leaven from previous baking, see To make a sourdough leaven, page 16.

Makes 2 round loaves

The leaven
* 60 ml/2 fl oz cold water
* walnut of leaven from previous baking
* 120 g/4 oz stoneground wholemeal flour
* pinch of ground cumin

The sponge
* 350 ml/12 fl oz warm water
* 15 g/^{1}/2 oz fresh yeast
* 425 g/15 oz unbleached white bread flour

The dough
* 300 g/10 oz unbleached white bread flour
* 2 teaspoons salt
* ^{1}/2 teaspoon bicarbonate of soda

1 To make the leaven, mix the water with the walnut of leaven. Add the wholemeal flour and cumin, and knead to a homogenous dough with your fingertips. Put it in a small bowl covered with clingfilm and leave to ripen in a warm place (24°C/75°F) for about 6-9 hours. It will at least double in size.

2 To make the sponge, mix the leaven with the water and the yeast to a soup, then add the 425 g/15 oz flour gradually, beating all the while. Give it at least 500 beats with the hand to really stretch the gluten. Leave in a covered bowl to rise at 21°C/70°F for anything up to 12 hours, but at least 2 hours. The longer it is left, the sourer it should be.

3 Mix the flour for the dough with the salt and bicarbonate of soda, then add it to the sponge. Mix to a dough, then turn out on to a floured work surface and knead very well for 10-15 minutes, until it clears.

4 Divide in two and mould each piece into a ball. Place on a slightly warmed and greased large baking sheet, or two if your oven is not big enough to take a large baking sheet. Cover with oiled clingfilm and leave to rise in a warm place (26°C/80°F) for 1 ^{1}/2 hours. They will spread and rise. Meanwhile, heat the oven to 230°C/450°F/gas 8.

5 Slash the loaves with cuts radiating from the centre, dust with flour and bake for 25 minutes, spraying the oven with water twice in the first 4 minutes. Reduce the temperature to 200°C/400°F/gas 6 and bake for about another 15 minutes, until the loaves sound hollow when tapped on the bottom. If the loaves spread and touch when proved on a single baking sheet, you can easily break them apart and check more reliably that they are cooked by pressing a finger into the exposed crumb. If the indentation does not spring back, they need more cooking. Cool the cooked bread on wire racks.

BOSTON BROWN BREAD

The early settlers of New England found growing wheat difficult: rye was easier in wet, northerly climates and on hungry, briefly settled lands. And 'Indian' corn - maize - the indigenous staple of north America, was easier still. Hence breads were often of mixed flours - as they had been among poorer households back in England - for instance, rye and wheat, or the 'thirded' breads made of wheat, rye and cornmeal.

Boston Brown Bread is one of these, and it also betrays its origins by being steamed, so simple to make in kitchens that had no ovens.

It is almost universal today to make Boston Brown Bread with bicarbonate of soda (not used until the second half of the 19th century) rather than yeast, and a healthy addition of molasses or treacle. This really makes it an aerated cake rather than bread as we understand it. It does go awfully well with Boston baked beans - another heavily sweetened savoury food.

To make this bread, you could use a 1 kg/2 lb pudding basin, as if making a Christmas pudding. However, most American cooks use an old tin can, emptied of coffee, baked beans or tomatoes, washed and well greased.

My favoured vessel is a straight-sided 1.2 litre/2 pint glass flask from a coffee maker. Grease it well with butter, and put a well-fitting disc of buttered greaseproof paper on the bottom before you put in the dough.

You will also need a small rack or trivet to keep the pudding basin, tin or flask from touching the bottom of the saucepan and, of course, a saucepan, with a lid, large enough to do the steaming.

Makes 1 loaf
* 90 g/3 oz cornmeal
* 90 g/3 oz wholemeal rye flour
* 90 g/3 oz wholemeal wheat flour
* $1/2$ teaspoon salt
* $3/4$ teaspoon bicarbonate of soda
* $1/2$ teaspoon cream of tartar
* 225 ml/8 fl oz milk and water, mixed half and half
* 90 ml/3 fl oz black treacle or molasses

1 Mix the cornmeal, rye and wheat flours, salt, bicarbonate of soda and cream of tartar together in a bowl. Warm the milk and water and dissolve the black treacle in it. Add the liquid to the flour mixture and bring together with a wooden spoon to a moist dough.

2 Grease a 1 kg/2 lb pudding basin or a 1.2 litre/2 pint tin or glass flask and line the base with a disc of greaseproof paper. Grease the paper and spoon the dough into the mould. It should be somewhat more than half-full. Cover the top of the mould with a double sheet of greaseproof paper, tied securely with a piece of string.

3 Lower it on to a trivet or rack standing in a large pan. Half fill the pan with hot water. Cover with a lid and bring to the boil. Steam for approximately 2 1/2 hours, checking periodically to make sure it has not boiled dry.

4 Once the bread is cooked, take the flask out of the water and turn it upside-down on a wire rack. After a minute or two, if you have greased it well enough and there are no obstructions or top lips, the loaf will drop down of its own accord. Remove it and leave the bread to cool on the rack. Eat this bread fresh.

NEW ENGLAND BUTTERMILK ROLLS

These little rolls have quite the finest crumb imaginable: perfect for a dinner party, as light as air, and not difficult to make. Small wonder that they have become popular in Old England as well as in the original home, made again by cooks wanting a bread suitable to go with rich and elaborate food. The instructions for making up the rolls may seem complex, but once mastered, are easily repeated.

Pinch one edge of each square of dough firmly together between work surface and thumb, then place each roll, pinched side down, in a greased cup of a Yorkshire pudding or bun tray.

Makes 8 rolls
* 15 g/¹/2 oz fresh yeast
* 200 ml/7 fl oz buttermilk, or plain yoghurt and water mixed half and half, at 38°C/100°F
* ¹/2 teaspoon honey
* 60 g/2 oz butter
* 375 g/13 oz unbleached white bread flour
* ¹/2 teaspoon bicarbonate of soda
* ¹/2 teaspoon salt

1 Crumble the yeast into the buttermilk, dissolve the honey in the mixture and leave to ferment in a warm place for 30 minutes.

2 Melt half the butter. Combine the flour, bicarbonate of soda and salt in a bowl, and add the liquid and melted butter. Mix to a soft dough, then turn out on to a floured work surface and knead for about 8 minutes, until perfectly smooth and resilient. Leave the dough to rise in a bowl covered with oiled clingfilm in a warm place (26°C/80°F) for about 1 hour, until doubled in size.

3 Turn out on to the lightly floured work surface, knock back and form a square cushion. Leave it to rest, covered, for 10 minutes. Roll the dough into an oblong, about 50 cm/20 inches long and 30 cm/12 inches wide. So as not to tear the dough, work slowly with breaks to give the gluten a chance to relax; otherwise, it will constantly be trying to spring back to its original size.

4 Melt the rest of the butter and brush it over the surface of the dough. Slice the oblong of dough lengthwise into six 5 cm/2 inch strips. Lay these strips on top of each other, flipping the last one over so that the butter side contacts the one below.

5 Cut this strip into eight squares. Pinch one edge of each square firmly together between work surface and thumb, then place each roll, pinched side down, in a greased cup of a Yorkshire pudding or bun tray. Leave them to prove in the warm for 1 hour, covering the tray with an inverted large bowl or something similar. Meanwhile, heat the oven to 230°C/450°F/gas 8.

6 Bake the rolls for 15 minutes, until golden brown, then cool them on a wire rack.

SOUTHERN CORN BREAD

When the first European settlers arrived in north America, the native Indians had maize as their staple, a grain unheard of in Europe. The settlers took to this Indian corn as readily as did their Spanish predecessors in Mexico and the lands to the south. The American adoption of Indian methods and recipes, and their alteration to match European practice has given us some enjoyable loaves.

Soon the settlers were making corn pone (from the Algonquin *appone*) and Johnny cakes (perhaps named after the Shawnee tribe) as often as breads made from grains they had brought with them across the ocean.

Some recipes combined the old with the new - 'ryaninjun' is rye and Indian (corn) - others mixed maize with eggs to make almost a soufflé - and called it spoon bread. This particular recipe is as simple as can be, but perfect served hot with bacon in the morning.

The southern states of America prefer a white cornmeal, and would rather have their breads cooked thin, while in the north, yellow is the star, and thicker is better. Colour apart, there is no important difference between white and golden cornmeal.

Maize has no gluten at all. It will not rise or stretch like a wheaten or even a rye dough. This is why it is mixed with other grains if you want to make a more conventional loaf, for instance Portuguese Corn Bread, page 74. The alternative is a flat bread, made lighter with eggs or baking powder, or a combination of the two.

Makes one 22.5 cm/9 inch bread

* *150 g/5 oz medium or fine cornmeal (see Note)*
* *1 teaspoon baking powder*
* *1/2 teaspoon salt*
* *1 egg*
* *250 ml/9 fl oz milk*
* *bacon fat for greasing the frying pan*

1 Heat the oven to 230°C/450°F/gas 8 and then heat a 22.5 cm/9 inch ovenproof frying pan.

2 Mix the cornmeal, baking powder and salt together in a bowl. Mix the egg in the milk and pour the mixture on to the cornmeal. Stir to incorporate, then beat well to ensure the batter is absolutely smooth.

3 Grease the warmed frying pan with bacon fat, and pour in the batter carefully. Return it to the oven and bake the bread for about 15 minutes, until golden.

4 Slip the cooked bread out of the frying pan, slice it and eat hot with rashers of bacon.

Note: How finely the corn has been ground makes a difference to this recipe. If you can only locate coarse meal, or that sold for polenta in the Italian style, make it finer by whizzing it in your spice or coffee grinder.

OTHER BREADS

The idea of the large, risen loaf is unique to Europe and cultures dependent on it, for instance those of European Jews. The rest of the world tends to eat rice or some other staple, or cook breads that are flat even when they are leavened. One exception is the steamed bread of northern China. Otherwise, yeasted loaves have been baked as a result of exposure to Europeans.

Flatbreads like pitta, naan, chapatis, or parathas are, of course, delicious, and should be made as often as other sorts by the keen experimenter.

The means by which they are cooked may be more difficult to replicate; not everyone has a tandoor oven in their kitchen. Equally, there are grains and materials that are virtually unobtainable outside their own country - the fresh masa that is made into tortillas, or the *te'f* flour that is the basis of the Ethiopian injera, are two examples. In these cases, some approximation is necessary, though the results will be no less enjoyable.

Clockwise from centre top: *Ethiopian Wheaten Flatbread, Pitta Bread, Middle Eastern Lavash, Bagels, Challah.*

WEST INDIAN ROTI

After the abolition of slavery, the English plantations in the West Indies looked to other parts of the Empire for cheap labour. So it was that Indians took up residence, especially in the southern islands of Trinidad and Tobago, and the Guianas on the South American mainland. Their presence transformed the cookery of those parts: curries and pilaus were second nature; masalas and East Indian spices, universal flavourings. The new Indian settlers also brought their breads, and this is the origin of the West Indian roti, a variation of the Indian flatbreads, chapati and paratha. It is used in the same way: as a scoop for stews and curries, and as a bread to be eaten for its own sake. Sometimes the large roti are used as giant envelopes for a filling of curried goat, say, or the smaller ones are served whole, and small pieces torn off to dip and scoop into the bowl of food before you. This recipe is based on the excellent instructions in a classic of Caribbean cookery by Elisabeth Lambert Ortiz, *The Complete Book of Caribbean Cooking*.

Shape the layered quarter-circles into approximate rounds and roll out to 30 cm/12 inch discs again.

Makes 4 breads
* *225 g/8 oz unbleached plain white flour, or fine wholemeal chapati flour*
* *1 teaspoon baking powder*
* *1 teaspoon salt*
* *40 g/1 ¹/2 oz butter*
* *120-150 ml/4-5 fl oz water*
* *120 g/4 oz clarified butter, melted*

1 Mix the flour, baking powder and salt together in a bowl and rub in the butter. Make a well in the centre and add 120 ml/4 fl oz of the water. Mix to a dough, then add more water if necessary. It should be firm, but not too stiff. Turn the dough out on to a floured work surface and knead for about 4 minutes, until it is clear.

2 Leave in a covered bowl for 30 minutes, then turn out and knead again. Divide into four pieces, mould them into balls and roll with a rolling pin into 30 cm/12 inch discs. Brush the top surface with the melted clarified butter. Fold in half, then half again. Cover and leave for 20 minutes.

3 Shape these layered quarter-circles into approximate rounds and roll out to 30 cm/12 inch discs once more.

4 Heat a griddle, or heavy cast iron frying pan over medium heat. Cook each roti in turn. Cook on one side for 1 minute, then flip it over (some say it is best to use a wooden spatula) to cook the other side. Brush the top with clarified butter. Let it cook as it is for 2 minutes, then brush the top again. Cook for another minute. Turn over for the last time to finish off the topside until it browns.

5 The last thing to do is to break up the surface of the roti, so that it looks more like a paratha. Put the roti on a chopping board and hit it with a rolling pin until the outside layer flakes. Store wrapped in a tea towel until ready to eat.

TORTILLAS

Tortillas are flat breads made from maize: 'the knife, fork, plate and napkin' of Mexico, the staple of the Aztecs and Maya peoples in pre-Columbian times; 'the rest [of their diet] was sauce' comments a modern scholar. They developed an ingenious method of softening the dry kernels of corn by soaking and boiling them in lime-water before grinding to a paste. This was called nixtamal and is the raw material of fresh masa, from which tortillas are fashioned. Though freely available in Mexico and Latin America, fresh masa is not often exported. What we can buy is masa harina, the flour obtained by grinding after the masa has been dehydrated. It is not nearly so easy to make tortillas from masa harina as it is from fresh masa. Our efforts will not match the tortillas described by a Spanish conquistador in the 16th century that were prepared for Aztec nobles, 'so thin and clean they are almost like paper and translucent'.

Though Mexicans may be adept at making tortillas by slapping from one hand to the other, gradually increasing the diameter of the paper-thin disc as they go, the novice will find it less simple. One solution is to use a tortilla press, a small hand device that stamps out acceptable tortillas.

Another is to make tortillas from wheat flour, a speciality of northern Mexico and the south-western states of America. Enthusiasts quote an Indian proverb in their support: 'After tasting flour tortillas, the children cry for them as a man craves good whiskey.'

CORN TORTILLAS

Makes 12
* *225 g/8 oz masa harina*
* *300 ml/10 fl oz tepid water*

1 Mix the masina harina and water in a bowl, and bring together to a softish dough. Getting the right texture is all-important and will come with experience. Too wet and the tortilla will stick to hand, table or tortilla press; too dry and the dough will not hold together while you attempt to make it thin and broad. Old Latin American hands claim that the amount of water will vary according to the freshness of the masa harina, and even the state of the weather.

2 Divide the ball of dough into 12 pieces and roll these into small balls between the palms of your hands. This dough will not suffer from any amount of handling. Press each ball to make a small disc, then slap from hand to hand to extend it. Alternatively, place the disc on a clean surface (formica, for instance) and press it with the flat of a palette knife, turning it over at regular intervals to ensure it does not stick to the work surface. Continue until you achieve a tidy disc between 12.5 and 15 cm/5 and 6 inches in diameter.

3 Heat a dry griddle over medium heat, slip the discs on to the griddle and cook them on both sides, turning when the edges start to curl and the surface is flecked with brown. The Maya cooked them on flat stones heated in the fire, or on clay griddles called *comales*. As they cook, pile them one on the other between a clean cloth. Eat them warm, but they also can be reheated.

Note: In this recipe the tortillas are not salted, but you may add a good pinch of salt if you wish.

WHEAT TORTILLAS

Makes 12

* *300 g / 10 oz unbleached white flour*
* *1 ¹/₂ teaspoons salt*
* *1 ¹/₂ teaspoons baking powder*
* *60 g / 2 oz lard*
* *225 ml / 8 fl oz hot water*

1 Combine the flour, salt and baking powder in a bowl, and rub in the lard. Add the hot water and mix lightly to a soft but not runny dough. Leave to rest for about 20 minutes.

2 Divide the dough into 12 pieces and mould them into balls. Cover and rest. On a floured work surface, flatten each ball, then use a rolling pin to extend the disc to at least 15 cm/6 inches. Keep turning the dough so that it does not stick to the work surface.

On a floured work surface, flatten each ball of dough, then use a rolling pin to extend the disc to at least 15 cm/6 inches. Keep turning the dough so that it does not stick to the work surface.

3 Heat a dry griddle over high heat, slip the discs on to the griddle and cook them on both sides, turning them as soon as the surface starts to bubble, after less than a minute. Stack them up in the same way as Corn Tortillas (opposite).

GUATEMALAN SWEET BUNS

Pan buns

Makes 8 large buns
* 15 g/¹/2 oz fresh yeast
* 120 ml/4 fl oz warm water
* 450 g/1 lb unbleached white bread flour
* large pinch of salt
* 60 g/2 oz white sugar
* ¹/2 teaspoon ground aniseed
* 120 ml/4 fl oz coconut milk
* 8 drops of vanilla extract
* 1 egg
* 3 tablespoons corn oil

1 Cream the yeast in the warm water. Mix the flour, salt, sugar and ground aniseed in a bowl, and make a well in the centre. Add the yeast liquid and mix in a little of the flour with your fingers to make a sponge. Leave for 20 minutes, add the coconut, vanilla extract and egg to the bubbling sponge. Mix to a dough. Add the corn oil and knead it into a dough while still in the bowl. Turn out on to a lightly floured work surface and knead for 5 minutes.

2 Leave the dough to rise in a bowl covered with oiled clingfilm in a warm place (24°C/75°F), until doubled in size. Turn it on to the floured work surface and divide into eight pieces. Roll these with the flat of your hands into thin sausages about 40 cm/16 inches long. If the dough resists stretching, roll it in stages.

3 Shape each sausage into a spiral or snail, starting from the centre and working outwards. Pinch the end to the main body of the spiral so that it does not spring out. Leave them to rise under oiled clingfilm on a greased baking sheet for 30 minutes, until doubled in size. Meanwhile, heat the oven to 230°C/450°F/gas 8. Bake the buns on the centre shelf for 15-20 minutes, until evenly browned. Cool on wire racks.

PERSIAN FLATBREAD

Barbari

Makes 2 loaves
* 30 g/1 oz fresh yeast
* 250 ml/9 fl oz warm water at 32°C/90°F
* 450 g/1 lb white flour
* 1 teaspoon salt
* vegetable oil for brushing

1 Cream the yeast in the warm water. Put the flour in a bowl and make a well in the centre. Pour the yeast liquid into the well. Pour a little of the flour over the surface of the water and leave to bubble in a warm place (24°C/75°F) for 20 minutes. Add the salt to the sponge mixture and mix it all into a dough. Turn out on to a floured work surface and knead for 10 minutes, keeping the dough moist but not sticky.

2 Leave the dough to rise in a bowl covered with oiled clingfilm in a warm place for about 45 minutes, until doubled in size.

3 Turn out on to the lightly floured work surface and divide the dough in two. Work each piece into a ball, then roll into a long oval about 12 mm/¹/2 inch thick. Place on greased baking sheets, cover with oiled clingfilm and leave to prove in a warm place for 20 minutes. Meanwhile heat the oven to 220°C/425°F/gas 7.

4 Brush the loaves with oil and bake in the centre of the oven for about 20 minutes, until golden brown. Eat warm.

ETHIOPIAN WHEATEN FLATBREAD

Yesinde injera

Conventional baked breads in Ethiopia are called *dabbo*, but the injera, which is a soured pancake made from various grains, is the oldest and most traditional form. The staple grain of Ethiopia is a grass unique to the country called *t'ef* (*Eragrostis Abyssinica*). The nearest approximation we can achieve with grains available in Europe is millet. Different forms of millet, such as sorghum, are important staples for poorer countries in tropical Africa and Asia, although the breads made with such flour are not capable of normal leavening.

The recipe I have given here uses wheat, as being more acceptable to home bakers. Barley, millet, rice flour or cornmeal could equally well be tried. Many recipes now use baking powder or yeast to give a start to fermentation or aeration. I suggest using a piece of leaven to give a sour taste, as well as a piece of fermented yeast dough from any bread made the previous day, to aid fermenation.

Injera have to be made in a large frying pan when baking at home. Ethiopian cooks, however, will make them on a flat griddle laid over flames - much larger than anything we normally have in the kitchen cupboard. The injera is laid flat on a dish and fragrant stew (*wot* or *we't*) is piled in the centre for the eater to sample by means of tearing pieces of injera from the edge and using them as scoops.

Makes about 10
* *1 tablespoon leaven (see recipe, page 16)*
* *2 tablespoons of the previous day's dough*
* *1.35 litres/48 fl oz still spring water or boiled water*
* *700 g/1 1/2 lb stoneground brown (85% extraction) flour*

1 Mix the leaven, fermented dough and water together in a bowl. Add the flour to make a batter. Leave to stand at room temperature at least overnight, or for up to 24 hours, until it has risen and tastes sour.

2 Heat a large non-stick frying pan over medium heat. Pour about 175 ml/6 fl oz batter into the pan in a spiral pattern, starting at the edge and working clockwise until you reach the centre, then tip the pan so that the batter covers the bottom, like a pancake. Cook for 3-4 minutes. The edge will lift from the pan when it is ready. Take it out of the pan and cool on a clean tea towel while cooking the remainder.

Pour approximately 175 ml/6 fl oz of the batter into the heated pan in a spiral pattern, starting at the edge and working clockwise until you reach the centre.

BAGELS

The bagel is a Jewish bread, perhaps originating in Austria, migrating to Polish Galicia and thence to North America where it has become a standby of the Jewish delicatessen. The slightly enriched dough is shaped into rings, given a short rise, then poached for a matter of seconds before baking. The poaching makes the crust chewy rather than crisp, a texture reinforced by the short rising time. The crust may be brushed with egg to give gloss (an effect also achieved by putting sugar into the poaching water), and it may be coated with onion flakes, poppy seeds or sesame seeds.

Makes 10

* *15 g/¹/₂ oz fresh yeast*
* *2 teaspoons malt extract*
* *150 ml/5 fl oz tepid water*
* *300 g/10 oz unbleached white bread flour*
* *1 teaspoon salt*
* *2 tablespoons vegetable oil*
* *1 tablespoon malt extract for the poaching water*
* *1 egg white mixed with 1 tablespoon cold water for glazing*
* *poppy seeds or sesame seeds (optional)*

1 Combine the yeast, malt extract and the 150 ml/5 fl oz tepid water in a bowl and stir to dissolve. Mix the flour and salt together, form a well in the centre and pour in the yeast liquid, then the oil. Mix to a dough, then turn out on to a floured work surface and knead for 8 minutes. The dough will be quite soft and pliant.

2 Leave the dough to rise in a bowl covered with oiled clingfilm in a warm place (24°C/75°F) for about 1 hour, until doubled in size.

3 Turn it on to the work surface, divide into 10 equal sections and roll each of them into a neat and tidy ball. Rest them for 5 minutes covered with a clean cloth. To form the bagels, flatten each ball slightly, then pinch your thumb through the centre to the bottom. These rings can then be

made larger by playing hoopla with the bagel by twirling it round and round your thumb, or a forefinger. The hole in the middle of the bagel needs to be bigger at this stage than you want it to be at the end of cooking. As the dough rises, so the hole will shrink.

4 Leave to prove on a floured tray covered with a cloth for 10 minutes. Heat the oven to 220°C/425°F/gas 7 and bring a large saucepan of water with the malt extract added to it to the boil, then leave it simmering. When the bagels have proved, slip three or four into the hot water. Poach for 1 minute, then turn with a slotted spoon and cook the other side for 30 seconds. Remove and drain on a clean tea towel.

5 Once they have all been poached, place the bagels on a greased baking sheet and brush with the egg white glaze. Bake in the oven for about 30 minutes, until golden brown.

Slip the bagels, three or four at a time, into the pan of water and malt extract. Poach for 1 minute, then turn with a slotted spoon and cook the other side for 30 seconds.

PITTA BREAD

Makes 8
* 15 g/ ^{1}/$_2$ oz fresh yeast
* 225 ml/8 fl oz tepid water at 21°C/70°F
* 400 g/14 oz unbleached white bread flour
* 2 teaspoons salt
* 1 tablespoon olive oil

Top: Pitta Bread.
Bottom: Middle
Eastern Lavash.

1 Dissolve the yeast in the water in a large bowl. Mix the flour and salt and add them gradually to the liquid, beating vigorously. Mix the flour really energetically for at least 8-10 minutes to condition it. Add the olive oil and mix once more. Turn the dough out on to a floured surface and knead for 5 minutes.

2 Leave the dough to rise in a bowl covered with oiled clingfilm for approximately 1 ^{1}/$_2$ hours, until doubled in size. Bring the dough together on a well-floured work surface. Divide it into eight pieces and form them into balls. Leave to rest for 5 minutes, then roll into flat ovals about 5 mm/^{1}/$_4$ inch thick. Leave them to prove in a warm place between two floured tea towels for about 20 minutes. Meanwhile, heat the oven to 230°C/450°F/gas 8 and warm one or two greased baking sheets.

3 Slip the breads on to the sheet or sheets and bake for approximately 6 minutes. It is not intended that they should colour, so more than one shelf may be used in the oven at one time, but the heat must be intense enough to cause them to puff up (the result of steam forcing the two halves of the bread apart, which is one reason for the initial dough being moist). Cool briefly on wire racks, then wrap them in tea towels to keep the crusts soft. Eat them warm.

Variation: 'Family size' pitta breads can be made by dividing this amount of dough into four pieces. The cooking time will need to be slightly longer.

MIDDLE EASTERN LAVASH

Lavash is the crisp flatbread found universally through Arab and Near Eastern countries. It needs the same dough as naan, but it is rolled thinner so that it bakes crisp. Lavash can be made and stored, like a crispbread.

Makes 6-8
* *175 g/6 oz of the previous day's dough*
* *175 ml/6 fl oz plain yoghurt at room temperature*
* *1 teaspoon salt*
* *7 g/^{1}/4 oz fresh yeast*
* *225 g/8 oz unbleached white bread flour*

1 Put the previous day's dough in a bowl with the yoghurt, salt and yeast. Mix with a wooden spoon until entirely smooth. Add the flour gradually, mixing vigorously until it is a moist and supple dough. Turn out on to a floured work surface and knead for 10 minutes.

2 Leave the dough to rise in a bowl covered with oiled clingfilm in a warm place (24°C/75°F) for between 2 and 3 hours, until tripled in size.

3 Turn out on to the lightly floured work surface, knock back lightly and divide into six or eight pieces. Form them into balls and leave to rest on the side of the table. Meanwhile, heat the oven to its maximum temperature, at least 230°C/450°F/gas 8, and warm some greased baking sheets.

4 Roll out each ball to an oval as thin as possible (taking into account the size of your oven). You may need to rest each piece in the middle of rolling out so as to relax the gluten and lessen the resistance to the rolling pin. Transfer the lavash to a warm baking sheet as soon as rolling is completed, and bake, without turning, for approximately 5-6 minutes. Cool, then wrap in a cloth if going to be kept.

113

CHALLAH

Challah is bread for the Jewish sabbath: a luxury wheaten loaf to mark the holy day, to set it apart from the incessant work of the rest of the week - and a daily diet of dark rye bread. Bread holds the key to much religious symbolism for Jews as for other communities. Challah was the dough set apart and given to the priests. This symbolic gift is still re-enacted - by the breadmaker of the house, or by the commercial baker. A portion of dough is abstracted before the final loaf is shaped, it is blessed and then burned to a cinder in the oven. In Middle Eastern cultures, the same ritual is thought to ward off the evil eye.

Challah is usually a braided or plaited loaf, witness perhaps to a medieval German origin of the bread we eat today (compare the Swiss Plaited Loaf on page 82), but this coiled shape is also traditional for the celebration of the Jewish New Year - its roundness symbolizing the fullness of time.

The luxury implicit in the bread is gained from butter and eggs (though not all recipes have these). A golden colour - inside and out - has also been ever popular. Some bakers add saffron to the dough to accentuate this.

Makes 1 large loaf
* 2 eggs and tepid water in a jug, to measure in total 225 ml/8 fl oz
* 1 tablespoon honey
* 15 g/¹/2 oz fresh yeast
* 450 g/1 lb unbleached white bread flour
* 1 teaspoon salt
* 60 g/2 oz unsalted butter
* 1 egg yolk beaten with a little water for glaze
* 1 teaspoon poppy seeds or sesame seeds (optional)

1 Put the eggs and tepid water in a bowl, add the honey and yeast, and stir to dissolve. Mix the flour and salt in a bowl and rub in the butter. Make a well in the centre and pour in the yeast liquid. Mix to a soft dough, then knead on a lightly floured work surface for 5 minutes.

2 Place the dough in a bowl with a piece of oiled clingfilm pressed to the surface, to prevent skinning, and leave to rise at room temperature for about 3 hours.

3 Turn out on to the lightly floured work surface and knead for 5 minutes. Return the dough to the bowl, cover again and leave to rise a second time in the warm (26°C/80°F) for between 1 and 2 hours, until at least doubled in size.

4 For the final shaping, gently roll the dough into a sausage about 40-50 cm/16-20 inches long, taking care not to tear the skin on the 'top' side and showing no joins from the turning and rolling. Make a simple coil, pinching the end to hold the shape in the oven. Place on a greased baking sheet, cover with oiled clingfilm and prove at 26°C/80°F for about 1 hour. Meanwhile, heat the oven to 200°C/400°F/gas 6.

5 Brush the loaf with the egg yolk glaze and scatter with the poppy or sesame seeds, if using. Bake on the middle shelf of the oven for 30-40 minutes. It should feel very light and sound hollow when tapped. Cool on a wire rack.

Place the dough on a greased baking sheet and shape it into a simple coil, pinching the end to hold the shape in the oven.

NAAN

There are a host of breads from India, some leavened like this naan, others not, like chapatis and parathas. Naan is the white bread of the Muslim north-west, of Punjab and Kashmir and, beyond that, Afghanistan and central Asia. The large breads in restaurants are cooked in tandoors - beehive domes arching over a charcoal brazier on the floor of the oven, with food being introduced through an opening at the top. When making bread, the cook slaps the sheet of dough on to the side wall. It hangs down over the flame in the pit, one end stuck to the wall, the rest forming a huge tear shape below. Households, even in India, do not usually have tandoors, so home produced naans are then cooked in a conventional oven, under a grill, or over charcoal

The writer Helen Saberi, who lived and cooked in Afghanistan, has eloquently described naans made for her. While most recipes suggest a simple yeast dough, or sometimes a yoghurt fermentation, she noticed that many Afghan naans were made with a sourdough, or at least a fermentation based on a piece of dough saved from the previous day's baking. This gives the bread an excellent sharp flavour which brings out the best of the taste of the flour. While Indian breads are often made with fine white flour (Indian wheat is quite strong and suitable for breadmaking), Afghani baking is usually done with finely ground wholemeal, similar to chapati flour, which could be used in this recipe.

Makes 2 large breads or 4 smaller ones
* 175 g/6 oz of the previous day's dough, kept back, covered, in the cool
* 175 ml/6 fl oz plain yoghurt, at room temperature
* 1 teaspoon salt
* 7 g/^{1}/4 oz fresh yeast
* 225 g/8 oz unbleached white bread flour

1 Put the previous day's dough in a bowl with the yoghurt, salt and yeast. Mix with a wooden spoon until entirely smooth. Add the flour gradually, mixing vigorously until it is a moist and supple dough. Turn it out on to a floured work surface and knead for 10 minutes. Leave the dough to rise in a bowl covered with oiled clingfilm in a warm place (24°C/75°F) for between 2 and 3 hours, until tripled in size.

2 Turn the dough out on to the lightly floured work surface and knock back lightly. Divide it into two or four pieces, form into balls and leave them to rest on the side of the work surface. Meanwhile, heat the oven to 230°C/450°F/gas 8 (or hotter, if possible) and warm some greased baking sheets.

3 Roll out each ball to an oval about 5 mm/^{1}/4 inch thick: if making two larger breads, the ovals will measure about 50 x 20 cm/20 x 8 inches. You may need to rest each piece in the middle of rolling out so as to relax the gluten and lessen the resistance to the rolling pin.

4 Transfer the naan to the baking sheets as soon as rolling is completed, and bake, without turning, for approximately 5-8 minutes. They should have taken colour and they may be crisp in parts. Once cooked, wrap in a cloth until needed, but eat them warm and fresh.

Variations: The naan can be brushed with ghee or clarified butter for an extra touch of luxury, and this may be enhanced with a sprinkling of spice or seed as well.

If you would rather cook the bread under a conventional salamander grill, you may find the smaller size more convenient to handle. Turn the breads halfway through the cooking unless you have a heavy grill pan which can be preheated.

ACKNOWLEDGEMENTS

I am grateful to Elizabeth Carter, Rolf Peter Weichold, Adam Nicholson, Angelika Noack, Crowdy Mill of Harbertonford, and many others for advice and assistance.

SELECT BIBLIOGRAPHY

Banfield, Walter: Manna (London, 1937)

Bateman, Michael, & Heather Maisner: The Sunday Times Book of Real Bread (Aylesbury, 1982)

Bürher, E.M., & W. Zehr: Le pain à travers les ages (Paris, 1985)

Calvel, R.: La Boulangerie Moderne (3rd edition, Paris, 1962)

Clayton, Bernard, Jr.: Bernard Clayton's New Complete Book of Breads (New York, 1987)

Collister, Linda, & Anthony Blake: The Bread Book (London, 1993)

Confederation Nationale de la Boulangerie: Mon Métier Boulanger (Paris, 1990)

David, Elizabeth: English Bread and Yeast Cookery (London, 1977)

Duff, Gail: The Complete Bread Book (London, 1993)

Edlin, A.: A Treatise on the Art of Bread-Making (London, 1805, reprinted 1992)

Field, Carol: The Italian Baker (New York, 1985)

Irons, J.R.: Breadcraft (n.d., ca.1935)

Kelly, Sarah: Festive Baking In Austria, Germany and Switzerland (Harmondsworth, 1985)

Kirkland, John: The Modern Baker, Confectioner and Caterer (London 1907)

Littlewood, Alan: Breadcraft (London, 1987)

Mesfin, D.J.: Exotic Ethiopian Cooking (Falls Church, Virginia, 1993)

Montandon, J.: Le bon pain des provinces de France (Lausanne, 1979)

Ortiz, Joe: The Village Baker (Berkeley, 1993)

Parmentier, Antoine Auguste: Le Parfait Boulanger (edition of 1788, Paris; reprinted Marseille, 1981)

Poilâne, Lionel: Faire son pain (Paris, 1982)

Poilâne, Lionel: Guide de l'amateur de pain (Paris, 1981)

Time-Life Books: Breads (Amsterdam, 1980)

INDEX

INDEX